Analytic Support to Intelligence in Counterinsurgencies

Walter L. Perry, John Gordon IV

Prepared for the Office of the Secretary of Defense
Approved for public release; distribution unlimited

RAND NATIONAL DEFENSE RESEARCH INSTITUTE

The research described in this report was sponsored by the Office of the Secretary of Defense (OSD) and conducted within the International Security and Defense Policy Center of the RAND National Defense Research Institute, a federally funded research and development center sponsored by the OSD, the Joint Staff, the Unified Combatant Commands, the Department of the Navy, the Marine Corps, the defense agencies, and the defense Intelligence Community under Contract W74V8H-06-C-0002.

Library of Congress Cataloging-in-Publication Data is available for this publication.

ISBN 978-0-8330-4456-3

Cover photo by U.S. Air Force Technical Sergeant John M. Foster; courtesy of the Department of Defense

Published 2008 by the RAND Corporation
1776 Main Street, P.O. Box 2138, Santa Monica, CA 90407-2138
1200 South Hayes Street, Arlington, VA 22202-5050
4570 Fifth Avenue, Suite 600, Pittsburgh, PA 15213-2665
RAND URL: http://www.rand.org/
To order RAND documents or to obtain additional information, contact
Distribution Services: Telephone: (310) 451-7002;
Fax: (310) 451-6915; Email: order@rand.org

Preface

Operations in Iraq and Afghanistan have shown that U.S. forces need more-effective techniques and procedures to conduct counterinsurgency. Beyond the experience in these two countries, it is likely that U.S. forces will face similar, irregular warfare tactics from future enemies that are unwilling to engage in conventional combat with U.S. forces. This suggests the need for a well-structured systems analysis process to address the insurgent threat as it is evolving in Iraq and Afghanistan and to assist in the development of more-general approaches to such threats in future campaigns.

This monograph presents a broad range of analytic techniques that can be used to support the security portion of counterinsurgency operations. Its purpose is not to discuss the broader elements of counterinsurgency, such as nation-building and improvements to governance in nations threatened with insurgency. Instead, it combines research supporting two complementary studies: one focused on ways to improve U.S. counterinsurgency capabilities and a second aimed at developing operational analysis techniques to defeat improvised explosive devices (IEDs).[1] The first study provides a framework for thinking about the nature of an insurgency and the latter then examines operational analysis techniques to answer the operational and tactical counterinsurgency questions that evolve at each stage in the insurgency.

[1] John Hollywood, Thomas Sullivan, Ryan Keefe, David Nealy, and Walter L. Perry, *Targeting IED Networks in Iraq*, Santa Monica, Calif.: RAND Corporation, forthcoming. Not releasable to the general public.

Both studies were conducted for the U.S. Department of Defense within the International Security and Defense Policy (ISDP) Center of the RAND National Defense Research Institute, a federally funded research and development center sponsored by the Office of the Secretary of Defense, the Joint Staff, the unified combatant commands, the Department of the Navy, the Marine Corps, the defense agencies, and the defense intelligence community.

For more information on RAND's ISDP Center, please contact the director, James Dobbins. He can be reached by email at james_dobbins@rand.org; by phone at 703-413-1100, extension 5134; or by mail at RAND Corporation, 1200 South Hayes Street, Arlington, VA 22202-5050. More information about RAND is available at www.rand.org.

Contents

Figures

Tables

Summary

Insurgency is one of the oldest forms of conflict. Records of ancient regimes show how their rulers were frequently faced with revolts and insurrection. The reality that insurgency is a continual problem has persisted into the modern era. The United States Army spent decades conducting what was, essentially, a counterinsurgency in the American West during the period after the Civil War; the British Army was faced with multiple insurgencies during the period of Empire in the nineteenth and early twentieth centuries; and as the colonial era came to an end in the post–World War II period, the Western militaries—especially their armies—continued to face this challenge. Today, the problem of combating insurgencies continues to loom large for the armed forces of several western nations.

Yet despite this, the preference of most Western militaries has been to focus on conventional combat operations against the armed forces of another nation state. This is reflected in the spending patterns of the NATO nations today. Compared with the money devoted to new systems for high-intensity combat, the amount invested in the preparation for irregular warfare pales. Of course, quality does not equal quantity, and a strict resource metric does not necessarily gauge emphasis. However, when we couple the money spent with the relative ability of nations to conduct conventional and counterinsurgency operations, it is clear that the emphasis is on conventional forces.

What is the reality that faces the Western militaries today? Iraq provides a useful example. Whereas the major combat operations phase in Iraq lasted some 23 days (from the time U.S. and UK forces crossed the border from Kuwait into Iraq to the last major battle in Baghdad on April 10, 2003) the counterinsurgency period has lasted some 1,700 days as of this writing. This is consistent with the norm of post-World War II insurgencies.

Although Iraq and Afghanistan will probably reduce the appetite of Western nations to engage in similar events without vigorous domestic debate, a strong case can be made that the Western militaries simply cannot turn their back on the study of and preparation for counterinsurgency in a manner similar to the way the conventional U.S. military turned its back on the study of low-intensity operations in the aftermath of the unfortunate experience in Vietnam. A major part of enhancing our ability to conduct counterinsurgency is improving our ability to analyze how insurgencies get started, the different nature of each individual insurgency, and the actions required by the security forces that are attempting to counter the movement.

This monograph examines the nature of the contemporary insurgent threat and provides insights on the need for better analysis of insurgency. It focuses on the security portion of a counterinsurgency effort. Other elements of counterinsurgency, such as efforts to improve governance in countries threatened by insurgency, are also critically important. However, those nonsecurity portions of counterinsurgency are beyond the scope of this analysis.

The Nature of Modern Insurgency

Today, theorists and doctrine writers, those in charge of training and equipment purchases, and the political leaders of the nations faced with insurgencies and other nations considering coming to their assistance must all consider the nature of modern insurgency. This is a profoundly important issue, since how nations view *insurgencies* will have significant influence on how their militaries and governments prepare for future *counterinsurgency* missions.

There is considerable discussion today about "what has changed." Does the modern, interconnected, networked, cable-television world obviate the lessons from past counterinsurgency campaigns? Or is the nature of insurgency so enduring as to render the recent phenomena of *jihad* just another chapter in what is a rather consistent story of how insurgencies develop and how they are countered? The reality is that there are important elements of truth in both views.

Whereas, in some respects, insurgencies have become slicker, quicker, and enabled by modern information technology, many of the principles of counterinsurgency operations remain fundamentally the same. This reality should strongly influence how today's Western militaries prepare themselves for the challenge. In all of this, we see the need for sound analysis in order to determine what capabilities and what mixture of new and old techniques are most appropriate for a particular insurgency.

Most insurgencies evolve over time. While occasionally an insurgency suddenly springs forth in a matter of months (this is essentially what happened in Iraq), in most cases insurgencies gradually gather strength—assuming they survive their initial, weak, proto-insurgency phase. In this early phase, the most effective government counters to the insurgents are generally intelligence services and the police. There may be little, if any, role for the military at this point.

If an insurgency survives past this initial stage, it can evolve into a small-scale insurgency. Now the insurgents start to make their presence felt with more-open propagandizing and occasional attacks against government forces and facilities. While the police and intelligence agencies remain in the lead to combat the insurgents, at this point there may be a need to involve the military in the effort, since the police may need help in some areas.

Should the rebels continue to grow in numbers and capability, it could become a large-scale insurgency. At this point, major portions of the country could be under insurgent control and a large portion of the population will have sided with the rebels. If the problem has reached such proportions, the insurgents stand a good chance of prevailing. On the government side, the military has by now probably taken the lead, since the insurgency is so strong that it is now beyond the ability of the police to control.

The Dominance of Intelligence

Although there are some similarities, the role of intelligence in conventional combat operations differs considerably from its role in support of irregular warfare, including insurgencies. Because the enemy in an insurgency is elusive, unknown, and most likely indistinguishable from the general population, intelligence operations are crucial.

Intelligence Operations in Support of Conventional Combat

In conventional combat operations, the intelligence mission is primarily to respond to the requirements imposed by the campaign plan—in essence, military intelligence. In this case, intelligence tends to support operations. Commanders decide what objectives they will seek to attain, and intelligence supports both the decisionmaking process and additional information needed to support the selected course of action.

Analysis in support of conventional operations is generally well understood. For example, operational analysis can help commanders sift through the intelligence data by systematically applying systems analysis techniques to the process of selecting the best course of action.

Intelligence in Support of Counterinsurgencies

Insurgent groups rarely resemble conventional force formations until they have wrested control of large amounts of territory from the government. They are usually made up of clandestine groups operating in the shadow world, disrupting activities of the government in ways that resemble criminal gangs. Little, if anything, is generally known about their order of battle, equipment, strategic goals, or tactics. In fact, their disruptive behavior can resemble the activities of ordinary criminals.

Successful intelligence operations in support of counterinsurgencies therefore resemble those of law enforcement agencies. Operations against these insurgent cells must depend upon the development of intelligence aimed at identifying cell members and their location. Insurgent command structures are also likely to be unconventional, and much effort must be expended on understanding the relationships among the members of the various groups involved in the insurgency.

Insurgents generally conduct acts of violence against the established government. Assassinations, bombings, kidnappings, and other forms of violence are common. Seemingly random acts against innocent civilians are conducted by insurgent gangs to intimidate and underscore the government's inability to protect the population. In investigating these incidents, considerable emphasis is placed on crime scene analysis, social network analyses, interrogation of detainees, forensics and biometrics. Military intelligence begins to resemble police intelligence.

Analysis in support of these police-like operations is likely to be considerably different than analysis to support conventional military operations. In supporting counterinsurgency operations, we need to apply existing, and perhaps new, analytic techniques to answer such questions as the following: Who are the insurgents? What are their objectives? Where will they strike next? How are they organized? Notice that answers to most of these questions are already known in conventional military operations. The law enforcement community often employs pattern analysis techniques, such as geographic profiling, to understand past criminal behavior and to predict where criminals are likely to strike next. This is something we explore here as well.

The Analytic Questions

Analysis in support of counterinsurgencies (indeed, in support of most unconventional wars) centers on contributing to intelligence production by focusing on required information elements. Because this is a unifying theme, we refer to analytic support in these cases as *intelligence analysis*. It is therefore important that we fully understand the anatomy of insurgent attacks. Figure S.1 depicts a typical sequence, from financing operations to conducting the attack. At each event in the chain, the insurgents are vulnerable to government detection and attack, but to varying degrees.

Figure S.1
The Insurgent Attack Event Chain

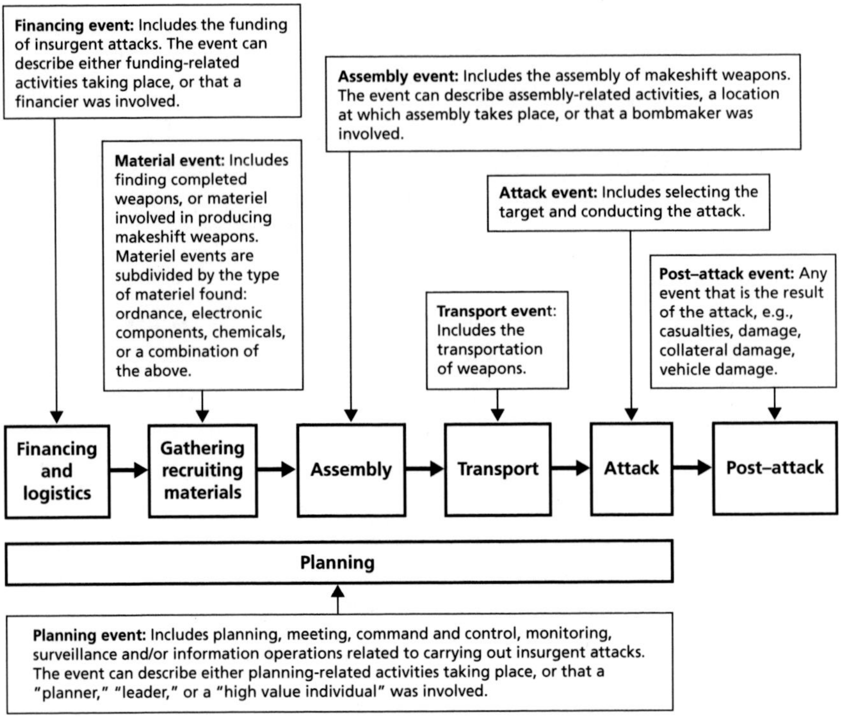

RAND *MG682-S.1*

The analytic questions at each stage in an insurgency therefore center on understanding what is needed to interrupt insurgent attacks at each point in the event chain. Some of these questions are the following:

- **Signs of a Nascent Insurgency.** What is the typical signature of a nascent insurgency—in terms of actions, pronouncements, and so on?
- **Leadership and Membership.** Who are the leaders and principal deputies of each insurgent group? Where are they located? What is the relation among the group members and between groups?

- Insurgent Goals. Are the insurgents striving to overthrow the existing government or to gain autonomy for a region? How can the government take advantage of each goal?
- **The Nature of Insurgent Attacks.** Where are the weapons caches used by the insurgents? Where are the next attacks likely to occur? What is the nature of the attack "event chain"? What foreign entities (governments or groups) are assisting in the attacks in some way?
- **Intelligence Sources.** How can we best leverage information obtained from detainees? How can we use forensic and biometric evidence to locate insurgents?
- **Financing and Recruitment.** Who is financing the insurgency? How are the insurgent groups recruiting members? What part of the population is susceptible to recruitment? What are the inducements to join?
- **Weapons.** What types of weapons are being used? Where do they come from? Where are they cached? Where are the assembly facilities for makeshift weapons? How are weapons delivered to attackers? Which groups are conducting the attacks?
- **Friendly-Enemy Interactions.** What operational patterns are friendly forces exhibiting? How is this behavior being exploited by the enemy? How can a friendly force alter its behavior to make its patterns more difficult to discern? If its patterns are discerned, how can a friendly force make it more difficult for the enemy to exploit?

For the United States and other friendly nations to come to the aid of a neighbor threatened by insurgents, it is important to answer these questions. To do so, we turn to intelligence analysis using some of the traditional tools of operational analysis and adding a few new tools.

In the process of applying these techniques, it is important to keep in mind two distinguishing characteristics of insurgencies: (1) When carrying out operations, insurgents are likely to subordinate global objectives to local objectives, and (2) any attempts by the friendly forces to counter insurgent attacks are generally met with counters to the counters—that is, insurgents are adaptive.

Analysis

The analytic tools needed to answer the research questions will be a mix of existing methods of analysis, some new approaches and perhaps different ways to apply existing methods. We suggest several analytic techniques based on our experience supporting operations in Iraq and Afghanistan. Not all have proven successful, but in some cases that may be because they have not yet been applied.

All analysis depends on data, and analytic support to counterinsurgency operations is no exception. The major source of information on enemy activities is generally a report that records "significant" activities. A significant activity can be any incident deemed important. For example, locating a weapons cache is a significant activity as is an enemy attack on a friendly convoy. In many cases, the most important pieces of information are recorded in narrative remarks sections—and not in the more structured data entries. Reports therefore are dependent upon the diligence of the individual soldier preparing the entry. In addition, there are other issues relevant to the usefulness of the data.

- **Data Collection.** Most data are collected to support operations—not to inform analysis.
- **Unevenness in Reporting.** Which incidents are considered "significant" can vary with the experience of the reporting unit.
- **Multiple Databases.** In Iraq and, to some degree, Afghanistan, the several databases are not linked or cross-referenced. Many are stored locally and not easily accessed.
- **Lack of a Standard Lexicon.** A critical requirement for database searches is that the terms used be consistent. Unfortunately, only recently have standard definitions begun to be applied to data entries in Iraq.

- **Friendly Data Generally Not Captured.** Most of the data collected in Iraq and Afghanistan are associated with enemy activities—little information is recorded about friendly operations.
- **Sharing Intelligence Data Among Agencies.** All too often, bureaucratic procedures inhibit or prohibit the sharing of information—much of which may be time-sensitive—between the organizations that are attempting to deal with the insurgency. Sharing intelligence information among allied nations is also difficult. This is particularly problematic for analysis.

Finally, we address some of the techniques that appear to show some promise of being useful to intelligence analysis in support of counterinsurgencies.

- **Discerning Patterns.** Some of the research questions can be answered only in terms of what we refer to as indicators—that is, what friendly units should look for when searching for enemy activity. The most frequently used methods to develop indicators are pattern classification methods, hierarchical decision trees, and linear discriminant analysis. All these methods examine factors associated with the occurrence of an event and then examine evidence in the form of training vectors to narrow the factors to a few strong indicators.
- **Predictive Analyses.** Predictive analyses aim at forecasting where (and sometimes when) the enemy will strike next. In the absence of data on friendly behavior, these techniques invariably depend upon statistical analysis of past insurgent behavior under the assumption that the past is prologue. The predictions therefore are based solely on what the enemy forces have done in the past—not on any interaction between friendly and enemy forces. Most assume an underlying randomness associated with enemy behavior. Although several of these predictive methods exist, very few are currently being used in Iraq or Afghanistan. Local commanders therefore resort to heuristic methods that rely on the location and timing of past insurgent attacks plotted on maps. To be effective (and accepted by commanders in the field), predictive meth-

ods should (1) recognize that insurgent attacks are not random, (2) provide a mechanism for grouping historical events, (3) account for an adapting enemy, (4) benefit from input from local commands, (5) recognize that analysis is local, like the insurgency, and (6) be better than what the command is presently using.

- **Analyzing Insurgent Networks.** Much of what commanders face across all phases of an insurgency consists of clandestine groups of loosely connected individuals carrying out criminal acts against the government and the friendly forces supporting it. In Iraq, commanders at all levels devote considerable time understanding the relationships among key people in the cities, towns, and villages within their areas of operation. For insurgents to successfully carry out the activities depicted in Figure S.1, they must be in contact through some form of network. Understanding the structure of these networks is therefore a primary goal of counterinsurgency operations. A possible solution is the development of an intelligence-based common picture of the insurgent networks that (1) uses the most current intelligence estimates, (2) is automated so as to provide access to multiple commands, and (3) can be easily updated.
- **Friendly-Enemy Interactions.** In general, friendly forces are attacked because they are exposed in some way. In an insurgency, unlike in conventional combat, there are no "lines of contact" behind which friendly forces are secure. Typically, friendly forces create safe enclaves from which to mount operations. Once out of the enclave, friendly forces are exposed and therefore vulnerable to enemy attack. Because friendly forces cannot hide their activities, the enemy is free to attack—provided it has the resources and sufficient time to plan. We explore two closely connected methods to examine the research question associated with friendly-enemy interactions: game theory and change detection.
- **Enemy-Friendly Interaction Analyses: A Game Theory Approach.** One advantage of using game theory is that the mental process involved in determining the payoffs forces us to assess enemy objectives: a favorable payoff to the enemy (Red) implies that it has achieved some part of its objectives. In a counterinsurgency,

friendly forces (Blue) make many decisions when planning and executing missions. They choose routes, times, travel speeds, and so forth. The set of Blue strategies corresponds to the set of possible realizations of these choices. Insurgent elements (Red) make their own decisions about attacking Blue. In general, the success of a Blue mission and the outcome of a Red attack depend on how well-matched Red's strategy is to Blue's strategy. Red must attack when and where Blue will travel, and may need to adjust its tactics in a way that is tuned to the given Blue mission. We assume that the outcome of the game for Red can be measured in terms of the expected payoff to be derived from the consequences of Red propaganda, friendly casualties, etc. Crucially, the analysis does not depend on actually measuring the payoffs. One approach is to examine relative payoffs. For example, Red may conclude that it has achieved its objective better with more Blue casualties than with fewer. The assumption is merely that the payoffs could be evaluated on some ordinal scale.

- **Enemy-Friendly Interaction Analysis: Response Detection.** A study currently being led by the Center for Naval Analyses (CNA) examines a unit's historical movement patterns using archived Blue Force Tracker (BFT) data.[1] This is generally a graphical process whereby BFT data are plotted on a map of the unit's area of operation—outside its forward operating base. This is repeated for a subsequent time period of equal length, and the difference is calculated. In areas where significant change is observed, the analysis focuses on enemy activity to see how the enemy has exploited (responded to) the change in friendly behavior. Next, area density changes are computed within grids overlaid on the area of operations, and along road segments within those grids if more resolution is needed. An important aspect of this type of analysis is the development of suitable measures and metrics that reflect the level of Red-Blue interaction from one time period to the next. For the friendly forces, operational density is appropriate, i.e., the

[1] The work presented here summarizes research conducted by Dr. Caryl Catarious, a research analyst at CNA.

levels of Blue force activity per unit area or per unit kilometer. For Red, the metrics are simply the activity of interest for the analysis being conducted: the number of friendly-force casualties per time period, the number of attacks of specific types or all types per time period, the number of weapons caches found and cleared per time period, and so forth. The goal of the response detection analysis is to focus on areas where (1) a significant change in Blue force activity has been observed, and (2) insurgents have either successfully taken advantage of the change or have failed to do so.

Conclusion

Our goal in this monograph has been to examine how operational analysis can be used to support the security portion of counterinsurgency operations. Insurgencies evolve over time. Normally starting as a small, clandestine movement of "true believers," insurgent movements are usually very weak and vulnerable in their early stages. If the movement survives and begins to grow, it can become a large-scale insurgency that has a reasonable chance of succeeding.

Our understanding of modern insurgency is evolving and improving. In some respects, the lessons and techniques used in past counterinsurgency efforts remain valid today. In other areas, important changes have taken place, especially in the ability of insurgents to use modern global information and communications networks to recruit, spread propaganda, organize, and control their operations.

As analysts engaged in trying to understand and assess modern insurgencies, we must realize that this is a different form of conflict from what we grew accustomed to during the Cold War and the 1990s, when most of us focused on the interaction of conventional military forces. Instead of merely conducting operational analysis, we are really engaged in using operational analysis techniques to support intelligence operations.

Acknowledgments

The authors wish to acknowledge the insights and assistance provided by a number of individuals. RAND is currently engaged in several counterinsurgency-related studies, including work on the IED challenge in Iraq and Afghanistan. Several of the key concepts in this monograph were adopted from existing and ongoing work from those studies. In particular, Daniel Byman, a RAND adjunct who is the director of the Security Studies Program at Georgetown University, has developed important insights on how insurgencies evolve, including the important proto-insurgency stage. RAND colleagues Joel Predd, Thomas Sullivan, and John Hollywood helped develop and apply some of the analytic methods described in this monograph. In addition, Caryl Catarious at the Center for Naval Analyses developed and applied the graphical response assessment methodology described in the text. The authors also wish to thank Stephen Kirin at the MITRE Corporation for his review of an earlier version of this monograph.

Abbreviations

BFT	Blue Force Tracker
CBRN	chemical, biological, radiological, and nuclear
CEXC	Combined Explosives Exploitation Cell
CIDNE	Combined Information Data Network Exchange
CNA	Center for Naval Analyses
COIN	counterinsurgency
COINCOP	Counterinsurgency Common Operational Picture
EOD	explosive ordnance disposal
FOB	forward operating base
GPS	Global Positioning System
IED	improvised explosive device
IPB	intelligence preparation of the battlefield
ISR	intelligence, surveillance, and reconnaissance
MNC-I	Multinational Command–Iraq
PIR	prioritized information requirement
PRT	provincial reconstruction team
SIGACTS	significant activities
SNA	social network analysis
TEDAC	Terrorist Explosives Device Analytical Center
TTP	tactics, techniques, and procedures
UAV	unmanned aerial vehicle

CHAPTER ONE

Introduction

Insurgency is one of the oldest forms of conflict. Records of ancient regimes show that their rulers were frequently faced with revolts and insurrection. The mighty legions of Rome spent more time suppressing insurgency within the Empire's borders than they did attempting to expand the limits of Rome's control. The reality that insurgency is a continual problem has persisted into the modern era. The U.S. Army spent literally decades conducting what was, essentially, a counterinsurgency effort in the American West during the period after the Civil War. The U.S. Marine Corps' primary mission in the decades before and after World War I was the protection of American interests and suppression of insurgency in various Caribbean nations. The British army was faced with multiple insurgencies during the period of Empire in the nineteenth and early twentieth centuries. As the colonial era came to an end in the post–World War II period, Western militaries—especially their armies—continued to face this challenge. Whether in Malaya or Kenya, Algeria, or Vietnam, the problem of combating insurgencies loomed large for the armed forces of the United Kingdom, the United States, France, and many other nations.[1]

[1] For a good overview of U.S. counterinsurgency campaigns from the earliest years of the Republic up to Iraq and Afghanistan, see Max Boot, *The Savage Wars of Peace*, New York: Basic Books, 2002.

The Focus on Conventional Operations

Despite insurgency's long history, the preference of most Western militaries has been to focus on conventional combat operations against the armed forces of another nation state. Indeed, the "corporate culture" of most Western armies, navies, and air forces is strongly biased toward preparation for major combat operations. That is certainly reflected in the spending patterns of the NATO nations today. Compared with the money devoted to new systems for high-intensity combat—whether aircraft carriers, fighters, armored fighting vehicles, or sensors intended primarily to locate and identify the platforms of an opponent—the amount invested in the preparation for "low-intensity combat," "irregular warfare," "counterinsurgency," or whatever term one wishes to use, pales in comparison. Of course, quality does not equal quantity and a strict resource metric does not necessarily gauge emphasis. However, when we couple money spent with the relative ability of nations to conduct conventional and counterinsurgency operations, it is clear that the emphasis is on conventional forces.

The Hard Lessons of Iraq and Afghanistan

What is the reality that faces the Western militaries today? Take Iraq, for example. Whereas the major combat operations phase in Iraq lasted some 23 days (from the time U.S. and UK forces crossed the border from Kuwait into Iraq to the last major battle in Baghdad on April 10, 2003) the counterinsurgency period has lasted 1,700 days as of this writing. This is consistent with the norm of post–World War II insurgencies. Of some 90 insurgencies in that period, the average length is about 13 years, with some, such as the long-standing conflict in Angola, lasting up to three decades. This is significant: The Iraq experience clearly shows that the patience of U.S. and European nations is finite and not open-ended—yet these conflicts, by their very nature, are lengthy struggles fought out in both the military and political arenas. Additionally, it may be difficult to determine when—or if—an insurgency has ended. For example, when severely threatened by government forces, insurgents may temporarily cease their activities and wait for a more opportune time to restart their campaign.

Although Iraq and Afghanistan will probably reduce the appetite of Western nations to engage in similar events without vigorous domestic debate, a strong case can be made that the Western militaries simply cannot turn their back on counterinsurgency in a manner similar to the way the U.S. military turned its back on the study of low-intensity operations after the unfortunate experience in Vietnam. The struggle against radical Islamists will simply not go away in the near term, whatever the outcome in Iraq and Afghanistan. Therefore, the Western militaries should make appropriate moves toward improving their ability to conduct counterinsurgency operations, rather than considering Iraq and Afghanistan as aberrations and one-offs. A major part of enhancing our ability to conduct counterinsurgency is improving our ability to analyze how insurgencies get started, the different nature of each individual insurgency, and the actions required by the security forces that are attempting to counter the movement.

About This Monograph

We first examine how insurgencies evolve over time and the changing role of government security forces (police, intelligence, and military) during the various stages of an insurgency. This depiction of how insurgencies grow sets the stage for the subsequent discussion of how the analytical needs of the counterinsurgent forces changes over time. Importantly, throughout the monograph we stress the need for high-quality intelligence in the counterinsurgency (COIN) effort, and the similarity of COIN to police work.

CHAPTER TWO

The Nature of Modern Insurgency

Today, theorists and doctrine writers, those in charge of training and equipment purchases, and the political leaders of the nations faced with insurgencies and other nations considering coming to their assistance must all consider the nature of modern insurgency. This is a profoundly important issue, since how nations view *insurgencies* will have significant influence on how their militaries and governments prepare for future *counterinsurgency* missions.

There is considerable discussion today about "what has changed." Does the modern, interconnected, networked, cable-television world obviate the lessons from past counterinsurgency campaigns? Or is the nature of insurgency so enduring as to conclude that the recent phenomena of jihad is just another chapter in what is a rather consistent story of how insurgencies develop and how they are countered? The reality is that there are important elements of truth in both views. Certainly, near-instant global communication gives insurgents unprecedented opportunity to agitate and propagandize on a global scale. In the case of the Islamic jihadis, they are able to spread their message that the entire Islamic world—the ummah—is under assault by "Western crusaders and their Zionist allies." Using the Internet and friendly or unwitting global media as their communications means, the jihadis can spread their message and recruit. Indeed, today insurgents and terrorists can essentially create their own "media network" by exploiting the Internet, using it to propagandize and spread their message. It is no longer possible for authorities to clamp down on the news coming from a region threatened by an insurgency. This is an important technological change—and it clearly influences the counterinsurgency response.[1]

At the same time, much about insurgencies and counterinsurgency responses remains the same. The age-old truisms: (1) the insurgents and the government are competing for the loyalty of the people; (2) lethal force must be used with considerable care in counterinsurgency operations; (3) the key role of military force in counterinsurgency operations is to provide a secure environment so that needed political and economic reforms and development can take place; (4) if the insurgents are cut off from support of the people, the insurgency will ultimately collapse; and (5) if the insurgents obtain sanctuary and support from nearby nations the challenge of counterinsurgency is greatly increased are still valid today—as they were when the blue-painted Scots could cause trouble and then flee back to their sanctuary in the Highlands on the other side of Hadrian's Wall, or when the Vietcong could propagandize about the corruption and brutality of the Saigon regime from their safe havens in Cambodia and Laos.

Whereas, in some respects, insurgencies have become slicker, quicker, and enabled by modern information technology, many of the principles of counterinsurgency operations remain fundamentally the same. This reality should strongly influence how today's Western militaries prepare themselves for the challenge. In all of this, we see the need for sound analysis to determine what capabilities and what mixture of new and old techniques are most appropriate for a particular insurgency.

Most insurgencies evolve over time. While they occasionally spring forth suddenly in a matter of months (this is essentially what happened in Iraq), in most cases, they gradually gather strength—assuming they survive their initial, weak, proto-insurgent phase. Figure 2.1 depicts the evolution of most insurgent movements.

---

[1] David C. Gompert, *Heads We Win: The Cognitive Side of Counterinsurgency,* Santa Monica, Calif.: RAND Corporation, OP-168-OSD, 2007.

Figure 2.1
The Evolution of an Insurgency

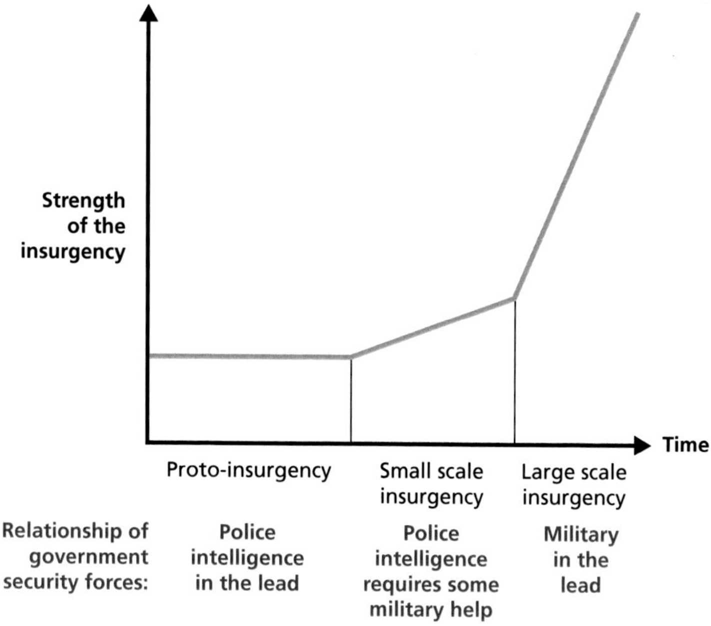

RAND *MG682-2.1*

Proto-Insurgency

In the initial, proto-insurgency phase, the movement is small and weak. It is normally composed of a small cadre of "true believers" who are strongly committed to dramatic change in the political-economic status quo of a nation or region. At this stage their capabilities—including their potential to "make trouble"—are limited. There may be different groups with somewhat similar agendas (e.g., the overthrow of the existing government), but these embryonic groups may actually be at odds with each other. At this early stage of an insurgency, the main concern of the insurgents is to survive. Indeed, most insurgencies collapse at this stage: They are swept up by the authorities or they simply implode after failing to gain sufficient support to expand. The initial leaders of the movement are trying to clarify their message and to recruit loyal and trustworthy companions. While some initial propagandizing is probably taking place (which may be essential to attract others to the cause), it is still relatively low-key and clandestine. This proto-insurgency phase could last years, as did the Marxist cells in Eastern Europe and Czarist Russia in the late nineteenth and early twentieth centuries, or in the early formative years of al-Qaeda.[2]

At this stage, the paradox for the authorities is that, while the insurgents are not much of a threat, they are also hard to detect. The very nature of the movement in this early phase—small, clandestine—means that it may not even be on the government's radar screen at all. The activities of the group may not even have crossed into the realm of the illegal. If they are noticed, group members could easily be mistaken for common criminals or essentially harmless crackpots. On the other hand, if the authorities *do* recognize the group as a budding insurgency intent on eventually overthrowing the government—and if they can find the leaders—this is precisely the easiest point at which the insurgency can be nipped in the bud. One factor contributing to the survival of small, proto-insurgencies is that, in some cases, the threatened government may deny that an insurgency even exists and attempt either to ignore the problem or to ascribe it to a small group of unimportant crackpots or criminals.

At this stage in the insurgency, the most important and applicable tools at the government's disposal are the police and its intelligence services. In many past insurgencies the police have been the first line of defense against the rebels. The police know the local communities and personalities to a far greater extent than the military forces do—at least in most nations. The closeness of the police to the community, plus the investigative strengths and inclination of most police forces,

[2] Whether al-Qaeda qualifies as a global insurgency is still debated. Some argue that it represents a global, radical, movement within Islam. Others ascribe to it the qualities of an insurgency, but one which has global aspirations.

means that they are an ideal agency to detect and penetrate small, clandestine insurgent groups. In this, the police can be greatly assisted by national (and possibly foreign) intelligence efforts that can use various means—technical, human sources, the ability to collect in nations that may be attempting to help the insurgents—to provide the police with vital information that could be the key to uncovering the insurgency at precisely its weakest point. Unfortunately, in too many developing countries the police are corrupt, politicized, or incompetent. Indeed, in some cases the brutality and corruption of the police can be a contributing factor that results in more support for the insurgents. In most nations, government military forces have little or no role at this early stage.

Small-Scale Insurgency

If the insurgency survives the proto-insurgency phase it can grow into a *small-scale insurgency*. At this point the insurgents will have gained sufficient numbers and strength to start to make their presence felt. Rallies led by insurgent leaders, open postings in public and on electronic media of calls to overthrow the corrupt government, small-scale attacks against government infrastructure, and occasional kidnappings and assassinations are hallmarks of this stage. The insurgents may have also been able to secure some amount of support from sympathetic groups outside the country, either friendly government or nongovernmental groups such as coreligionists or political fellow travelers. Diasporas can also be a source of strength and support for insurgent groups. Volunteers, funds, weapons, and political support from overseas ethnic, tribal, or religious communities that are sympathetic to the insurgents can help sustain and strengthen the insurgency.

What changes for the government at this stage of the insurgency? It is likely that the police and intelligence services will remain in the lead. The insurgents will still lack the capability to overthrow the government, although they will clearly be stronger than in the proto-insurgency phase. Therefore, the police should still have the advantage in most situations. However, there may be inadequate numbers of trained, loyal, police to provide adequate government presence in critical areas. In such circumstances, the insurgents will start to fill the vacuum that lack of adequate government security forces creates. If the insurgency continues to strengthen, the police may need growing amounts of assistance from military forces. The insurgents will almost always be able to choose when and where to make spectacular attacks. The sheer number of possible targets—power plants, transportation hubs, political figures, government buildings, for example—may mean that the police will simply lack the ability to provide security to all the most likely or important potential targets. Additionally, there may be situations where the insurgents are strong enough locally that the police require overt support from the military if they intend to move against a group of rebels.

Large-Scale Insurgency

Assuming that the threat is not defeated or contained, it proceeds into the large-scale insurgency phase. In this phase, the situation for the threatened government will have become quite serious. The insurgents by now have gained considerable support within the local population. Their numbers may be in the many thousands, and they will have reached a level of political and armed capability that gives them a distinct chance of succeeding. The success of the insurgents can now be used as "proof" of the viability of the movement, thus resulting in more local recruits and encouraging outside support from friendly governments and nongovernmental groups. Indeed, the fact that the insurgency has reached this level may be due in no small part to support provided by friendly "outsiders" in terms of money, volunteers, weapons, and political support and legitimacy.

The insurgents will now often be out in the open. They will have probably established physical control over various parts of the country and will likely be in a position to contest government control in other areas. If their objective is to establish an autonomous region broken away from control of the existing government, they will probably be well along that path. Whatever their ultimate political goal, the insurgents now have a good chance of prevailing.[3]

From the point of view of the government's intelligence and security forces, the roles of the military and police have almost certainly been reversed in this stage. Whereas the police were in the lead in the earlier stages, at this point the sheer strength of the insurgency will have probably forced the government to rely on its military—specifically its ground forces—to combat the insurgents. With insurgent groups well armed and numerous, the situation will have passed beyond the ability of the police to cope. While the police and intelligence organizations still play absolutely vital roles in the government's attempt to defeat the insurgents, the armed forces will probably be at the forefront of the counterinsurgency effort.

This changed situation highlights counterinsurgency's "paradox of force." Historically, when the forces of the government (or the insurgents themselves, in many cases) employ too much lethal force, the support of the population will often slip away. In this large-scale insurgency phase, when it is likely that military forces have to be committed to fight the more powerful insurgency, the possibility of heavy-handed use of force increases. Most military forces are not imbued with the ethic of "lethal force is the last resort," which is far more common in police forces. Militaries tend to be rather blunt instruments and are probably not nearly as familiar with local populations as are the police. Nevertheless, if the insurgency has reached this critical phase, there may be no option other than committing military force.

It tends to be in this last, major, phase of insurgencies when foreign forces are committed in large numbers, if they are committed at all. This was the case when the Soviet intervened in Afghanistan in 1979 and when the United States decided to commit considerable numbers of conventional ground combat units to Vietnam in 1965. Those decisions were made because it was believed that the local governments were on the verge of collapse and the only way to prevent imminent defeat was to pour large numbers of foreign troops into the

---

[3] See Daniel Byman, *Understanding Proto-Insurgencies,* Santa Monica, Calif.: RAND Corporation, OP-178-OSD, 2007.

situation, since a limited numbers of advisors had been shown to be inadequate.

The present situations in Afghanistan and Iraq are somewhat different because there were no local forces to be supported in those cases—they had already been swept away during the invasions of those countries. [4] This model is intended to portray how most insurgencies evolve over time. If the insurgents survive the vulnerable initial phase and start to gain strength, the relationship of the government's police and military forces will start to change. Understanding these phenomena will, through better analysis, help us defeat modern insurgencies. It is to this issue that we now turn.

---

[4] John A. Nagl, *Learning to Eat Soup with a Knife, Counterinsurgency Lessons from Malaya and Vietnam,* Chicago: University of Chicago Press, 2002; and Shelby L. Stanton, *The Rise and Fall of an American Army, U.S. Ground Forces in Vietnam, 1965–1973*, Novato, Calif.: The Presidio Press, 1985.

CHAPTER THREE

The Dominance of Intelligence

Although there are some similarities, the role of intelligence in conventional combat operations differs considerably from its role in irregular warfare, including insurgencies. Because the enemy in an insurgency is elusive, unknown, and most likely indistinguishable from the general population, intelligence operations are crucial. Analysis generally centers on developing evidence to support prioritized information requirements (PIRs)—what the commander needs to know to take action against the insurgents. Because it is important to understand how intelligence operations differ in counterinsurgency operations, we now compare intelligence in support of conventional and unconventional operations.[1]

Intelligence Operations in Support of Conventional Combat

In conventional combat operations, the intelligence mission is primarily to respond to the requirements imposed by the campaign plan—in essence, military intelligence. In this case, intelligence tends to support operations. Commanders decide what objectives they seek to attain, and intelligence supports both the decisionmaking process and additional information needed to support the selected course of action.

---

[1] See FM 3-24 and MCWP 3-33.5, *Counterinsurgency,* United States Army and United States Marine Corps, December 2006, Chapter 3, "Intelligence in Counterinsurgency."

First and foremost, the intelligence community is charged with creating the intelligence preparation of the battlefield (IPB). The IPB consists of a description of the enemy order of battle, enemy force disposition, terrain analysis, prevailing weather conditions, demographics within the area of operations, and much more. For a conventional opponent, the creation and updating of the IPB is feasible simply because the enemy is typically a state military force and is therefore known. Consequently, the IPB is able to provide the commander with a good sense of the enemy disposition in the battlefield. Sensor assets such as satellites, unmanned aerial vehicles (UAVs), and other forms of surveillance and reconnaissance are used to detect enemy formations and other pertinent features that enhance the IPB.

Once operations begin, the most important piece of information needed to support operations is enemy intent. Whether planning defensive or offensive operations, the commander studies the enemy's possible courses of action and charges the intelligence community to gather evidence to support the most likely of these. Therefore intelligence is asked to support operations. Commanders also rely on the intelligence community to help develop the possible courses of enemy action. The traditional reconnaissance and surveillance means for collecting intelligence are used. Enemy formations are rather easy to discern—even if camouflage is used—because the appearance of a conventional opponent's equipment and enemy forces is generally known.

Analysis in support of conventional operations is generally well understood. For example, operational analysis can help commanders sift through the intelligence data by systematically applying systems analysis techniques to the process of selecting the best course of action. Given the commander's objective and the courses of action under consideration, the analysts establish measures of effectiveness designed to assess the degree to which the objective is achieved and then examine the evidence (through mathematical manipulation or some subjective process) produced by the intelligence to recommend the best course of action.

Intelligence in Support of Counterinsurgencies

Insurgent groups rarely resemble conventional force formations. They are usually made up of clandestine groups (especially in the proto-insurgency phase) operating in the shadow world, disrupting activities of the government in ways that resemble criminal gangs. Little, if anything, is known of their order of battle, equipment, strategic goals or tactics. In fact, their disruptive behavior can resemble the activities of ordinary criminals.

Intelligence operations in support of counterinsurgencies therefore resemble more closely those of law enforcement agencies. Operations against these insurgent "gangs" must depend upon the development of intelligence aimed at identifying members and their location. Insurgent command structures are likely to be unconventional, and much effort must be expended on understanding the relationships among the members of the various groups involved in the insurgency. Unlike conventional combat operations, operations in an insurgency must depend upon intelligence before a course of action is decided on.[2] And even when good intelligence exists, decisionmakers must decide on one of three courses of action: kill, capture, or monitor. Which to choose depends, in part, on the recommendation of the intelligence community.

Insurgents generally conduct acts of violence against the established government. Assassinations, bombings, kidnappings, and other forms of violence are common. On occasion, seemingly random acts against innocent civilians are conducted by insurgent gangs to intimidate and underscore the government's inability to protect the population. Investigations of these incidents are generally conducted by law enforcement organizations. However, if the police are dysfunctional (as in Iraq), the investigation tasks fall upon the military. Consequently,

---

[2] This is underscored in the U.S. military's new counterinsurgency manual: "Counterinsurgency (COIN) is an intelligence-driven endeavor. . . . Commanders require accurate intelligence about [the populace, host nation and insurgents] to best address the issues driving the insurgency." Field Manual (FM) 3-24 and Marine Corps Warfighting Publication (MCWP) 3-33.5, *Counterinsurgency*, Washington, D.C.: Headquarters, Department of the Army and Headquarters, United States Marine Corps, December 2006.

considerable emphasis is placed on crime scene analysis, social network analysis, interrogation of detainees, forensics, and biometrics. Military intelligence begins to resemble police intelligence. The Combined Explosives Exploitation Cell (CEXC) in Iraq and Afghanistan is an example of an organization created to perform police-like investigations of remnants of violent acts—usually the detonation of improvised explosive devices (IEDs)—against the government and civilians.[3]

Analysis in support of these police-like operations is likely to be considerably different than support to conventional operations. In some ways, it resembles the analyses conducted by the young mathematician on the television series, Numb3rs. On this program, young Charlie Eppes examines evidence collected by investigators and brilliantly deduces the solution to crimes.[4] Of course, that is television, where miracles can happen. In the more-serious world of analytic support to counterinsurgency operations, we need to apply existing, and perhaps new, analytic techniques to answer such questions as Who are the insurgents? What are their objectives? Where will they strike next? How are they organized? Notice that, in conventional operations, answers to most of these questions are known. As in the television show Numb3rs, the law enforcement community often employs such pattern analysis techniques as geographic profiling to understand past criminal behavior and to predict where criminals are likely to strike next.

---

[3] The CEXC in Iraq was established in 2004 as a joint coalition activity. CEXC members are subject-matter experts in such varying fields as explosive ordnance demolition (EOD), bomb investigations, military intelligence, latent fingerprint processing, and forensics photography. CEXC collects evidence from crime scenes and performs forensic and biometric analysis on the remnants. If the work exceeds its ability, the remnants are sent to the Terrorist Explosives Device Analytical Center (TEDAC), a U.S. government forensics facility at Quantico, Virginia.

[4] In *Numb3rs,* an FBI agent recruits his mathematical genius brother to help solve a wide range of challenging crimes in Los Angeles using what are essentially pattern recognition skills.

CHAPTER FOUR

The Analytic Questions

Analysis in support of counterinsurgencies (indeed in support of most unconventional wars) centers on contributing to intelligence production. That is, most questions asked by commanders have to do with understanding enemy intentions, organization, objectives, force disposition and alliances. In addition, because confrontation with the enemy is not direct, commanders require intelligence on the possible location of the next attack, the type of attack expected, weapons caches, and so forth. Clearly, the unifying theme is obtaining actionable intelligence. Therefore, we refer to analytic support in these cases as *intelligence analysis*. At each stage in the evolution of an insurgency (as depicted previously in Figure 2.1), the commander has information requirements to prosecute the counterinsurgency campaign. We next outline some fundamental categories of information associated with the three stages of insurgency.

The Proto-Insurgency

During this early stage, merely realizing that a nascent insurgency exists is problematic. Indeed, the military is not likely to be involved at all. Nevertheless, it is critical that the agency responsible for maintaining security (law enforcement or some other agency) be aware of the possible existence of insurgent groups. Some of the important information elements for this stage are listed in Table 4.1, along with some related research questions. As we proceed to subsequent stages, many of the information elements persist (Tables 4.2 and 4.3).

Table .4.1
Proto-Insurgency Information Elements

Information Element	Research Questions
Signs of a nascent insurgency forming	What are the indicators of a forming insurgency? What is the typical signature (in terms of actions, pronouncements, etc.) of a nascent insurgency?
The number of possible insurgent groups	What are the indicators that signal the existence of multiple groups?
Group leadership and membership	How large is each group? Who are the leaders and principal deputies? Where are they located? What is the relation among the group members, between groups?
Insurgent goals	What are the insurgents' goals? Are they striving to overthrow the existing government or gain autonomy for a region? How can the government take advantage of each goal?
Assets and capabilities	How are the groups disseminating their messages? What is the principal nature of the violence committed by each group?

Small-Scale Insurgency

At this stage, it is known that an insurgency exists in sufficient numbers and strength to cause mischief. Messages begin to appear in all media to overthrow the existing government or to rally people to their cause. During this stage, the violence is likely to increase as the form and frequency of the attacks mature. Signs of alliances begin to appear among the detected insurgent groups, other countries sympathetic to their cause, and nongovernmental groups, such as coreligionists or political fellow travelers.

The increase in violence at this stage is calculated to intimidate and is therefore an important tool in the insurgents' efforts to broaden the insurgency. Table 4.2 lists the information elements associated with this stage. The attack event chain referenced in the table refers to the sequence of events that must take place for the insurgents to deliver ordnance on target. Figure 4.1 depicts a typical sequence starting with financing weapons to conducting the attack. At each event in the chain,

Table 4.2
Small-Scale Insurgency Information Elements

Information Element	Research Questions
The nature of the attacks	Where are the weapons caches used by the insurgents? Where are the next attacks likely to occur? What is the nature of the attack "event chain"? What foreign entities (governments or groups) are assisting in the attacks in some way?
The relationships among insurgent groups	What are the relationships among the various insurgent groups? What are the ideological differences among them that might be exploited?
Evolving group leadership and membership	How large is each group? Who are the leaders and principal deputies? Where are they located? What is the relation among the group members? What skills have been ascertained among group members?
Insurgent goals	What are the insurgent goals? Are they striving to overthrow the existing government or gain autonomy for a region? How can the government take advantage of each goal?
Information from detainees	How can we best leverage information obtained from detainees to counter insurgent attacks?
Evidence from forensic and biometric assessments	How can we use forensic and biometric evidence to locate insurgents and then to capture them, kill them, or monitor their activities?
Assets and capabilities	What weapons systems and tactics, techniques, and procedures (TTP) are the insurgents employing?

the insurgents are vulnerable to government detection and attack, but to a varying degree. More on this will be presented in the last stage.

The events depicted in Figure 4.1 form a sequence that allows us to think about the nature of insurgent attacks. The vulnerability of the insurgents at each event in the chain depends upon the nature of the attack. For example, if the attack is the detonation of a roadside bomb, then the assembly event appears to be the most vulnerable because bombmakers, weapons, triggering devices, transportation, and emplacers must converge to a single location.

Figure 4.1
The Insurgent Attack Event Chain

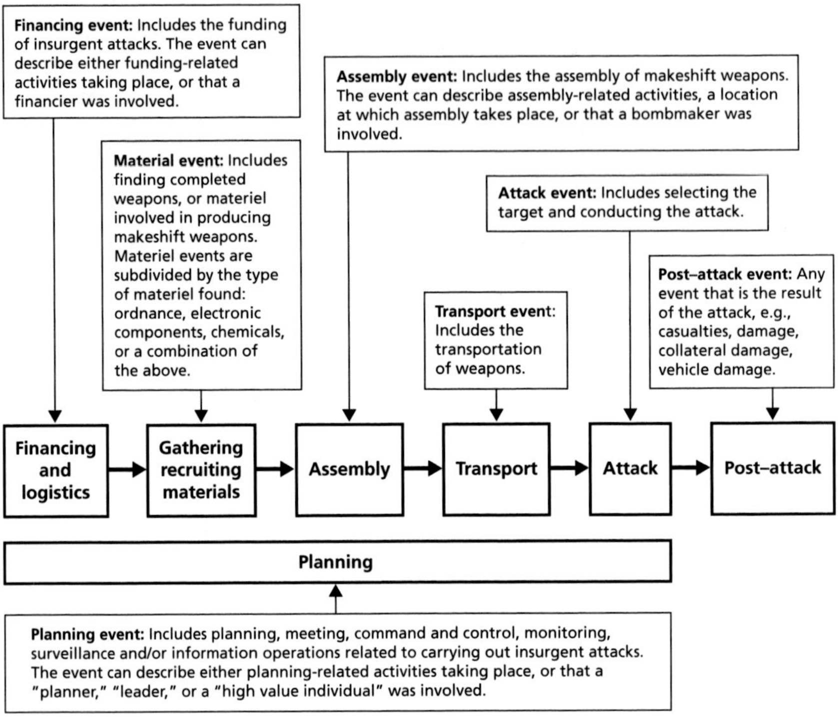

RAND *MG682-4.1*

Large-Scale Insurgency

In this phase, the situation has become so bad for the government that its very existence is threatened. The insurgents will have gained considerable popular support and will therefore be able to operate rather freely in the neighborhoods as they continue their attacks on government forces. We would also expect their attacks to have become more coordinated and sophisticated. It is likely that more-advanced and therefore more-deadly weapons will be used. The ability of the government to protect the population will have diminished considerably, further bolstering the insurgents' cause. At this stage, understanding the attack event chain (Figure 4.1) becomes critical in that it is important to know where to interdict it to best advantage. Table 4.3 depicts the information elements critical at this stage.

For the United States and other friendly nations to provide effective aid to a country threatened by insurgents, it is important that answers to these questions can be obtained. It is not likely that intervention will be needed in the proto-insurgency phase, but, as we demonstrate, because we are focusing exclusively on security issues, the research questions and the intelligence information elements vary only slightly from stage to stage. To answer the questions, we turn to intelligence analysis, using some of the traditional tools of operational analysis and adding a few new tools.

Before we proceed, however, it is important to note two distinguishing characteristics of recent insurgencies that affect how we apply analytic tools to answer the research questions.

- *Insurgent activity is localized.* When carrying out their operations, insurgents are likely to subordinate global objectives to local objectives. This can be seen in Iraq today. The nature of the battle two streets away is likely to differ from what is happening on this street. That is because insurgencies are much like criminal activities where gangs control neighborhoods, not cities. Thus, the application of analytic tools must also be localized—thereby multiplying the analytic problem.[1]
- *Insurgents are adaptive.* As we have seen in Iraq and Afghanistan, any attempt by the coalition forces to counter insurgent attacks is generally met with counters to the counters. Most insurgent attacks are accomplished using low-tech weapons, so adapting is generally rather easy. For example, when the coalition deployed sophisticated jammers to Iraq to thwart radio-controlled IED triggering devices, the enemy adapted by turning to other means, such as infrared trig-

---

[1] Clearly, terrorists groups such as al-Qaeda have more-global objectives, but the various insurgent groups in Iraq and Afghanistan are much more locally focused.

Table 4.3
Large-Scale Insurgency Information Elements

Information Element	Research Questions
The nature of the attacks	Where are the weapons caches used by the insurgents? Where are the next attacks likely to occur? What foreign entities (governments or groups) are assisting in the attacks in some way?
The relationships among insurgent groups	What are the relationships among the various insurgent groups? What are the ideological differences among them that might be exploited?
Evolving group leadership and membership	How large is each group? Who are the leaders and principal deputies? Where are they located? What is the relation among the group members? What skills have been ascertained among group members? What networks (communications and other) are the insurgents using?
Insurgent goals	What are the insurgent goals? Are they striving to overthrow the existing government or gain autonomy for a region? How can the government take advantage of each goal?
The attack event chain	Who are the insurgency financiers? How are the insurgent groups recruiting members? What part of the population is susceptible to recruitment? What are the inducements to join? What types of weapons are being used? Where do they come from? Where are they cached? Where are the assembly facilities for makeshift weapons? How are weapons delivered to attackers? Which groups are conducting the attacks?
Information from detainees	How can we best leverage information obtained from detainees to counter insurgent attacks? And forensic evidence to counter insurgent attacks?
Evidence from forensic and biometric assessments	How can we use forensic and biometric evidence to locate insurgents and then to capture them, kill them or monitor their activities?
Friendly-enemy interactions	What operational patterns are friendly forces exhibiting? How is this behavior being exploited by the enemy? How can the friendly force alter its behavior to make its patterns more difficult to discern? If its patterns *are* discerned, how can the friendly force make it more difficult for the enemy to exploit?
Assets and capabilities	What weapons systems and TTP are the insurgents employing?

gering devices.[2] The implication for analysis centers on the half-life of the solutions offered. For example, predictive methods (see Chapter Five) that do not incorporate a model to deal with enemy adaptation should be based on recent history so as to capture adaptations to predicted attack locations. In other words, analysis must be temporally local assuming we concede that a model for adaptation is elusive.

---

[2] Stewart Magnuson, "Adaptive Foe Thwarts Counter-IED Efforts," *National Defense*, January 2006.

CHAPTER FIVE

Intelligence Analysis

The analytic tools needed to answer the research questions posed earlier are a mix of existing methods of analysis, some new approaches, and perhaps different ways to apply existing methods. What follows is a discussion of several techniques that might be used, based on our experience in supporting coalition forces in Iraq and Afghanistan. Our emphasis is on suggesting what we consider to be plausible techniques designed to attack the research questions posed earlier. To our knowledge, not all have proven successful, but in some cases that may be because they have not yet been applied.

Data: Precision Versus Accuracy[1]

The Multinational Command Iraq's (MNC-I) major source of information on enemy activities in Iraq is the significant activities (SIGACTS) report.[2] For this reason, the discussion that follows is based on the characteristics of the data contained in this database and other related data sources. Other sources of data in enemy activity may be available in Iraq, but only the SIGACTS data are used by MNC-I.

A significant activity can be any incident deemed important enough to record. For example, locating a weapons cache is a signifi-

[1] This discussion is based, in part, on a briefing given by the U.S. Joint IED Defeat Organization titled "Operational Analysis and the Counter-IED Fight," March 2007.

[2] SIGACTS are recorded online at the brigade level. The online system is called the Combined Information Data Network Exchange (CIDNE).

cant activity, as is an enemy attack on a friendly convoy. Like many databases, the SIGACTS database allows for the reporting unit to enter narrative remarks. In many cases, the most important pieces of information are recorded in these remarks sections—not in the more-structured data entries. Consequently the SIGACTS data are dependent upon the diligence of the individual soldier who prepares the entry. In addition, several other issues are relevant to the collection, completeness, and therefore usefulness of the data.

- **Data Collection.** Most data are collected to support operations—not to inform analysis. Consequently they vary in terms of quality—accuracy, timeliness, completeness, consistency, and so forth. Convincing commanders to collect additional data or to collect existing data in a format more amenable to analysis is usually difficult. However, because commanders benefit from useful analysis-generated intelligence, they are generally more disposed to do so.
- **Unevenness in Reporting.** Which incidents are considered "significant" can vary with the experience of the reporting unit. Early in their tour, units report that they record most incidents, no matter how minor. Later in their tour, reporting may be less frequent. This of course, can seriously affect analysis.
- **Multiple Databases.** In Iraq and to some degree in Afghanistan, the several databases are not linked or cross-referenced, and many are stored locally and not easily accessed. For example, the CEXC database mentioned earlier contains forensic data concerning some of the incidents in the SIGACTS database.[3] Typically, explosive ordnance disposal (EOD) personnel are called to the scene of an insurgent attack to examine the remnants of the attack. Whereas the original SIGACTS report was recorded by the unit experiencing the attack at the location indicated on their Global Positioning System (GPS) reading, the CEXC team may enter an entirely different location based on its reading because it

[3] Not all significant incidents are investigated by CEXC teams.

is at the exact site, whereas the unit may have moved some distance before taking a location reading.

- **Lack of a Standard Lexicon.** A critical requirement for database searches is that the terms used be consistent. If a search is made for all "indirect mortar attacks" against forward operating base alpha for example, it is important that every entry labeled "indirect fire attack" is indeed the same type incident however defined and that other entries not labeled "indirect fire attack" are not included. Unfortunately, it has only been recently that standard definitions have begun to be applied to data entries in Iraq.
- **Friendly Data Generally Not Captured.** Most of the data collected in Iraq and Afghanistan are data associated with enemy activities. We know quite a bit about what the enemy has done, but very little about the activities of the friendly forces. In general, this is acceptable for conventional combat operations because information on friendly activities is not critical except for reporting status. However, in an insurgency, it is crucial that we know a bit more about what friendly units are doing. For example, if we observe that the number of direct fire attacks are increasing, we can draw two conclusions: (1) The enemy has generally stepped up its attacks independent of friendly force activity, or (2) the friendly force is more exposed (i.e., out of forward operating bases [FOBs] for longer periods), thereby inviting stepped-up attacks. If we were able to capture the number of hours a unit spends outside the FOB during a given time period, the ratio—i.e., the number of direct attack incidents this time period/hours outside the FOB this time period—might illustrate the consequences of more or less exposure.
- **Sharing Intelligence Data Among Agencies.** Often there will be multiple agencies involved in collecting information about the insurgents and the population they are attempting to win over. Too often, bureaucratic procedures inhibit or prohibit the sharing of information—much of which may be time-sensitive—among the organizations that are attempting to deal with the insurgency. Sharing intelligence information among allied nations is also difficult. This is particularly problematic for analysis. Often, data

cannot be shared with analysts simply because the latter are not perceived as representing the interests of the agency holding the data.

Good analysis depends, in large part, on good data. In a counterinsurgency, analysis is designed to provide the commander with intelligence concerning the likely future behavior of the enemy. To do this, good data are critical. That said, the situation is not as bleak as one might expect based on the preceding discussion. Units in Iraq and Afghanistan have steadily improved their data collection—to include an increasingly rich set of friendly-force data made available through saved BFT reports and records kept at the unit level. However, as the coalition forces turn over control of provinces in Iraq, data collection and visibility into events on the ground are expected to diminish.

Discerning Patterns

Some of the research questions posed in Tables 4.1, 4.2, and 4.3 can be answered only in terms of what we refer to as *indicators*—what friendly units should look for when searching for such enemy activity as weapons caches, assembly sites, transportation routes, financiers, and so forth. There are several ways to derive useful indicators using traditional operational analysis techniques. The most frequently used are pattern classification methods, hierarchical decision trees, and linear discriminant analysis. In all these methods, the analyst examines factors associated with the occurrence of an event and then looks at evidence in the form of training vectors to narrow the factors to a few strong indicators. As an example, we illustrate the process through the use of a heuristic pattern classification technique.

Suppose we are interested in locating weapons caches in an area of operations. The first step is to identify the factors that may contribute to the decision to locate a weapons cache. For example, we would assume that insurgents would want to locate a cache where it is unlikely to be discovered by friendly forces. This suggests such factors as proximity to a school, a church or mosque, or location in a private home.

In addition, the cache should be accessible to the insurgents. This suggests additional factors, such as proximity to a road, railway, or waterway. Finally, insurgents would also be concerned with the safety of the cache. That is, the site selected should be such that accidental detonation of the stored weapons is precluded. This suggests such factors as controlled temperature, adequate storage space to minimize stacking, and so forth. Table 5.1 summarizes the factors one might consider in locating a weapons cache.

The objective is to classify a given location as either a likely weapons cache or not. To do this, we examine the data available on located weapons caches to narrow the set of factors to a few indicators. Locating a weapons cache is a "significant activity" and therefore, in Iraq, it is recorded in the SIGACTS database. The task now is to assess how similar or "close" the weapons cache location entries are to each other in terms of the factors we have identified.

One way to do this is to calculate proximity using a distance metric. Each qualifying entry can be structured as a vector of factor values. Next, weights are empirically derived from the existing data set for each of the factors. These weights measure the relative importance of each factor

Table 5.1
Weapons Cache Location Factors

Factor	Subfactors
Security	Distance to nearest school Distance to nearest mosque Distance to nearest hospital Home of known insurgent
Accessibility	Distance to nearest road Distance to railway station Distance to port
Safety	Presence of climate-controlled facility Presence of large storage facility

in classifying a location.[4] Once the weights have been calculated, a Bayesian classification algorithm is applied as follows:

1. Calculate a square matrix of distance differences using an appropriate weighted distance metric.
2. Create a class probability density for each class to be considered. That is, calculate the probability that an observation (set of observed factor values) is actually a weapons cache. This is done by summing the distances from each known member of the class (weapons cache) to the candidate observation and dividing that value by the total database entries in the class.[5] In this case there are only two classes: "weapons cache" and "not a weapons cache."[6] The set of classes might be richer if needed. For example, a cache may be mobile or stationary, large or small, a storage location for special purpose weapons (such as IEDs).
3. Calculate the posterior probability that the observation is a member of each class.
4. Assign the observation to the class for which it has the greatest posterior probability.
5. Finally, compare the assignment with the training set and adjust the weights such that a predetermined penalty function is minimized. Reiterate until the misclassification level is acceptable.

One of the features of this approach is that it allows the friendly commander to adapt to changing enemy tactics. The calculation of the weights can be an ongoing process that takes advantage of the most-

---

[4] For an explanation of how this is done, see Thomas Sullivan and Walter L. Perry, "Identifying Indicators of Chemical, Biological, Radiological and Nuclear (CBRN) Weapons Development Activity in Sub-National Terrorist Groups," *Journal of the Operational Research Society,* Vol. 55, 2004, pp. 361–374.

[5] It is also possible to employ a kernel to obtain a smooth estimate of the class density. In this case, we sum over the kernel of the distance.

[6] In the data, "found caches" are clearly identified as such. Caches not found are recorded in two ways: (1) if a mission to find a cache failed to produce one, and (2) all other entries in the database.

recent data so that when candidate factor values for a given observation are classified, the latest enemy tactic is accounted for.

Predictive Tools

An important role for intelligence in counterinsurgency operations is acquiring information concerning the insurgents' plans, that is, where they are likely to strike next (the attack block in Figure 4.2). Unlike in conventional operations where discerning enemy plans amounts to evaluating alternative courses of action, discerning enemy plans in an insurgency can be almost impossible at times because the enemy generally seizes opportunities to strike as they occur and because decisions occur at low levels and operations involve relatively few people and pieces of equipment. Hence, we need to know as much about what the friendly forces are doing as what the enemy plans to do.

Predictive analyses aim at forecasting where (and sometimes when) the enemy will strike next. In the absence of data on friendly behavior, these techniques invariably depend on some statistical analysis of past insurgent behavior , under the assumption that the past is prologue. The predictions are therefore based solely on what the enemy forces have done in the past—not on any interaction between friendly and enemy forces. Most assume an underlying randomness associated with enemy behavior. For example, an examination of past enemy attacks might reveal that the interarrival time of the attacks is exponentially distributed, leading to a Poisson distribution of the number of attacks per time interval. This is also true of the location of the attack. Thus we get an underlying bivariate Poisson distribution for the time and location of attacks.[7]

---

[7] The SCAN statistic, for example, is used to predict the spread of diseases. The assumption is that the timing and location of future outbreaks has a bivariate Poisson distribution. This turns out to be a reasonable assumption; therefore, the statistic is widely used in epidemiology. See for example, Martin Kulldorff, "Spatial Scan Statistics: Models, Calculations, and Applications," in *Scan Statistics and Applications*, Joseph Glaz and N. Balakrishnan (eds.), Boston, Mass.: Birkhäuser, 1999, pp. 303–322.

Although several predictive methods exist, very few are currently being used in Iraq or Afghanistan, and local commanders therefore resort to heuristic methods that rely on the location and timing of past insurgent attacks plotted on maps.[8] There are several reasons for this: Some of the predictive methods are extremely complex requiring knowledge of sophisticated software packages; some simply do not work in the environment in which they are required to perform; some provide information at a level of resolution that is simply too coarse for commanders to take action; and most cannot adapt to rapidly changing enemy tactics.

To be effective (and accepted by commanders in the field), predictive methods should possess the following characteristics:

1. *They should recognize that insurgent attacks are nonrandom.* Insurgent attacks are anything but "random" in time and location. Insurgents attack where friendly forces, civilians or static targets are (or will be) located and when they anticipate they will be at that location. For example insurgents emplace IEDs along roadways where it is anticipated that friendly forces will travel. Consequently any algorithm or mathematical process that purports to examine inter-arrival times or spacing of attacks is more likely to fail. The reason is that these lead to Poisson processes that are inherently random, even if they are described by a known distribution.
2. *They should provide a mechanism for grouping historical events.* For example, clustering is the process of organizing observations into groups that are similar in some way. In the case of insurgent attacks, similarity is usually taken to be "closeness." Clustering

[8] The Joint IED Defeat Organization has identified over 60 predictive tools. One of the problems with evaluating these tools is that they must be examined in the context in which they are to be used. That is, some tools may work well under some circumstances and at some tasks, but not in others. This suggests that there is no single best predictive tool, and that it may be fruitful to search for meta-methodologies for combining predictive heuristics and for tracking predictor performance over time. A study of the online learning paradigm has identified algorithms that are suited for just this purpose. Joel Predd, "Online Learning and IEDs: Exploring the Possibilities," RAND briefing, November 2006.

algorithms are capable of finding the structure in a collection of observations (time and location of historical insurgent attacks) and are therefore reasonably good predictors of future insurgent activity. Several types of clustering algorithms exist. One such algorithm is the K-Means Clustering algorithm. It is one of the simplest clustering algorithms and, although it has problems in application, it is easy to use.[9]

3. *They must account for an enemy that adapts.* If friendly forces are successful at predicting where the insurgents will strike next and they act on that intelligence, we would expect the enemy to react in some way so as to blunt the adverse effects of the friendly action. One way to counter this likely phenomenon is to examine more-recent historical events. Typically, analysts like to examine all the data possible to support whatever study they are conducting. When examining insurgent attacks, this means looking at all attacks that have taken place from the proto-insurgency period onward. However, what occurred six months ago may have no relevance to what will occur tomorrow. By shortening the time horizon, we are much more likely to capture enemy adaptations.
4. *Their development should benefit from input from local commands.* Regardless of how good the predictive technique may be, it will remain unused if the local commanders and their staff do not view it as helpful. This has been the fate of several techniques that were developed "in the laboratory" and delivered to the field with promise of spectacular success. The local unit is well aware of the history of insurgent attacks in its area of operations. Analysts need to tap into that knowledge when developing a predictive tool tailored to the unit's needs. In addition, it is helpful to hear from the units concerning the form the predictions are to take. Finally, the use of the predictive tool must

---

[9] See James B. MacQueen, "Some Methods for Classification and Analysis of Multivariate Observations," *Proceedings of the 5th Berkeley Symposium on Mathematical Statistics and Probability*, Vol. 1, pp. 281–297, Berkeley, Calif.: University of California Press, 1967. For a more complete treatment of clustering and classification see A. D. Gordon, *Classification*, 2nd ed., Chapman and Hall, 1999.

not overly burden the command: Required inputs should be at a minimum.

5. *They should recognize that, like the insurgency, analysis is local.* As we mentioned earlier, the nature of the insurgency can change from neighborhood to neighborhood in the same way that criminal gangs claim local territory. Consequently, our analysis must be local as well. We have already argued that, in order to capture the enemy's adaptation, we must base our analysis on recent history. This is also true of the area to which we apply our analysis. In Baghdad, for example, there are several factions in the religious and ethnic groupings that operate within neighborhoods only. And although they are loosely connected, they may have purely local objectives and therefore operate differently from other groups in the city.
6. *Scale matters.* One of the problems with predictive techniques is setting a balance between improving the likelihood that an attack will occur in the area nominated in the future and selecting an area that is small enough for a unit to successfully cover. Clearly, if we nominate the whole of Baghdad for a future attack, we are likely to be correct. However, this information is of little value to commanders on the ground fighting insurgents in more-confined area of operations. On the other hand, we can also nominate an area equivalent to a circle with a radius of 50 meters. This is clearly more manageable, but it is not as likely to include a future attack. In proposing a predictive tool, there is always tension between size and accuracy. Critics will always look at the likelihood of an attack in the nominated area as a measure of effectiveness of the predictive tool. We address this next.
7. *Is the predictive tool better than what the command is using now?* Because we desire an affirmative answer, this question can lead to favoring large predictive areas that have a greater probability of experiencing an insurgent attack. Local units have a good understanding of the events occurring in their area of operations. The intelligence centers at each unit will have maps of their area with past insurgent attacks plotted. In the absence

> of any predictive tools, the intelligence staff combines information from several sources to produce an estimate of where future attacks may occur. In other words, they manually create predictions. Any tool produced by an analyst therefore has to better than what they do now. Suggesting very large areas based on distant historical data is not likely to do the job.

Predictive tools that work and that are accepted by unit commanders as a good source of intelligence are certainly in demand. However, the analyst must understand that what he provides is just one piece of the greater intelligence picture within a rich intelligence environment. Frequently, the area nominated for likely future attacks is reduced by the intelligence staff based on other intelligence available to the command—and this is as it should be.

Finally, the commander must realize that although a nominated area does not guarantee the occurrence of a future attack, he should treat it much as picnickers treat a weather report: It is no guarantee of bad weather but they dare not ignore it.

Analyzing Insurgent Networks: The "Counterinsurgency Common Operational Picture" (COINCOP)

Across all three phases of insurgency, commanders face clandestine groups of loosely connected individuals carrying out criminal acts against the government and the friendly forces supporting it. In Iraq, commanders at all levels devote considerable time to understanding the relationships among key people in the cities, towns, and villages within their areas of operation. On whiteboards in almost every command operations center, there are hand-drawn networks depicting known or suspected relationships among insurgents in their areas. Unfortunately, these are purely local networks devoid of any consistency and generally not visible elsewhere.

For insurgents to carry out the activities depicted in the event chain in Figure 4.2, they must be in contact through some form of network. Understanding the structure of these networks is therefore a primary goal of counterinsurgency operations. A possible solution is the development of an intelligence-based common picture of the insurgent networks that (1) uses the most current intelligence estimates, (2) is automated so as to provide access to multiple commands, and (3) can be easily updated. One such tool might be something we term the "COINCOP."[10] The main function of a tool of this kind is situational awareness at all command levels. It might provide displays of key information about insurgent networks (and campaigns against them), including

- the insurgents, their assets and their personal relationships (including those with civilians)
- the location of insurgent cells, their weapons caches, and supply chains for weapons and other war-related equipment
- details of weapons and tactics used by the insurgents
- likely attack locations
- vulnerabilities, weaknesses, and targeting recommendations
- collaborative analysis and discussion of the insurgent networks and what strategies and tactics might work best against them
- planned and executed attacks against the networks.

To be effective, the COINCOP should present views for both commanders and analysts—most likely, intelligence analysts. The views must be tailored to the needs of each. COINCOP's main purpose beyond providing situational awareness is to show targeting opportunities against insurgent networks, show intelligence needs and collection opportunities, and help advise on force-protection decisions.

The concept, illustrated in Figure 5.1, includes four key display tools. The first presents views tailored to commanders, displaying the overall insurgent order of battle (to the extent that it is understood). It also displays key vulnerabilities of and threats to friendly forces and tracks current plans to attack the networks in various ways.

---

10 The concept presented here was developed by RAND colleague John Hollywood and it is described and applied to a real-world insurgency in *Targeting IED Networks in Iraq,* Santa Monica, Calif.: RAND Corporation, MG 568-OSD, 2008. This document is not releasable to the general public.

Figure 5.1
The COINCOP Concept Includes Four Display Tools

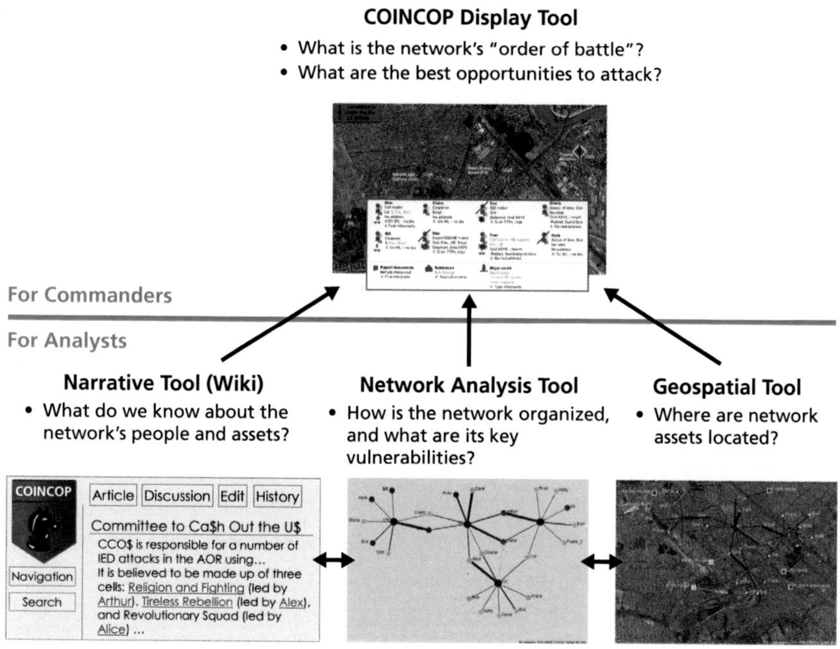

RAND *MG682-5.1*

Three additional tools support intelligence analysts. The first is a wiki or narrative tool. It provides encyclopedia-like entries on insurgent networks personnel, locations, and resources, as well as narrative histories of what the network has done and how it has been attacked to date. The wiki also provides discussion boards, allowing friendly force members to discuss their experiences in dealing with the network. Next, a social network analysis (SNA) tool is used to assess the network's organization and its key vulnerabilities (people whose loss would degrade network operations or whose interrogation would provide the most information about the network). Finally, the third analysis tool is the geospatial display. It plots key network locations, thereby facilitating attacks against them.

The COINCOP might be useful in informing decisions about directing strategic operations against insurgent networks. These decisions are aimed at setting the stage to receive target locations, especially from intelligence, surveillance, and reconnaissance (ISR) assets and the allocation and execution of these assets. The operations broadly relate to such activities as tasking informants, tasking tactical questioning and information operations, tasking monitoring operations and re-visit raids, and tasking interrogations and prosecutions. COINCOP has the potential to provide the information needed to make these tasking decisions.

However, as attractive as it might be, the COINCOP requires a considerable amount of data to be effective. It will likely be a monumental task to collect and process these data.

Enemy-Friendly Interaction Analyses

Another interesting characteristic of counterinsurgencies is the "action-reaction" phenomenon. In general, friendly forces are attacked because they are exposed in some way. In an insurgency, unlike in conventional combat, there are no "lines of contact" behind which friendly forces are secure. Typically, friendly forces create safe enclaves from which operations are mounted. In Iraq, these enclaves are the FOBs. In Afghanistan, provincial reconstruction teams (PRTs) are located throughout the country. When they are not conducting missions, the forces that make up these teams remain within heavily fortified bases. In either case, once off the enclave, friendly forces are exposed and therefore vulnerable to enemy attack. Because friendly forces cannot hide their activities, the enemy is free to attack provided it has the resources and sufficient time to plan.

Often, the friendly forces exhibit a pattern that is easily discernable to the enemy: Patrols depart and return at predictable times, they follow the same or a similar route each time, the composition of the patrol is roughly the same, and so forth. In some cases, they have no alternatives and are therefore forced to exhibit those patterns. For example, patrols must generally depart and return to their enclave from the same gate. Nevertheless, analysis can help the commander understand the patterns his forces are exhibiting and suggest how the unit might add some randomness to its operations.

There are four important research questions, all dealing with the interaction between friendly and enemy forces in an insurgency. Interactions between friendly forces and the insurgents mature as the insurgency matures. We listed the questions in Table 4.3 and record them here again for convenience:

1. What operational patterns are friendly forces exhibiting?
2. How is this behavior being exploited by the enemy?
3. How can the friendly force alter its behavior to make its patterns more difficult to discern?
4. If its patterns *are* discerned, how can the friendly force make them more difficult for the enemy to exploit?

As always, we start with the data needed to answer these questions. In this case, we need information on friendly operations and the record of enemy attacks against friendly forces. The latter is generally available in Iraq and Afghanistan through some form of SIGACTS. The former however, is more problematic. As mentioned earlier, data are generally collected to support operations and not analysis. This is particularly true of data on friendly forces. Units collect, for their own use, data on supply status, patrol movements, personnel status, and operations conducted and planned, but the data are rarely aggregated and are often discarded when no longer needed.

However, due primarily to operational experience in Iraq and Afghanistan, units are generally keeping better records of their activity and are archiving these records more regularly. Therefore, these data are now available to analysts. For example, BFT data are generally used to allow unit commanders to monitor their own and other friendly units.[11] These data were rarely recorded and stored for future analytic

[11] Blue Force Tracker records the location of vehicles every predetermined time period or distance traveled using either a GPS signal or a line-of-sight communication system. The vehicle must be fitted with the appropriate equipment to transmit its location. Other friendly units similarly equipped can then monitor the movement of the vehicles and have their own movement monitored.

purposes. That has changed recently, and BFT data are now available for analysis. In addition, units are recording other pertinent information and making it available to analysts. Although not perfect, this has greatly improved our ability to answer the first question above.

We have explored two closely connected methods to answer these questions. The first utilizes game theory and the second focuses on change detections. We look at game theory first.

A Game Theory Approach[12]

The use of game theory to analyze military operations is not new. Indeed, many game theory texts use examples from famous military engagements to illustrate the process.[13] Therefore, it is only natural that we examine its applicability to counterinsurgency operations or—to be more specific—friendly-enemy interaction analysis. One advantage of using game theory is that the mental process involved in determining the payoffs forces us to assess enemy objectives: A favorable payoff to the enemy (Red) implies that he has achieved some part of his objectives.

In a counterinsurgency, friendly forces (Blue) make many decisions when planning and executing missions. They choose routes, times, and speeds to travel, the spacing between vehicles in multi-vehicle convoys, and the configuration of various types of equipment (weapon systems) to be employed; the set of Blue strategies is in correspondence with the set of possible realizations of these choices. Insurgent elements (Red) make their own decisions about attacking Blue, choosing when and where to attack, which tactic to employ, and how to execute the attack; the set of Red strategies is in correspondence with the set of possible answers to these questions. Although this discussion suggests that a given strategy is associated with a single mission, we note that a single strategy could correspond to multiple missions.

---

[12] The work presented here summarizes research conducted by RAND colleague Joel Predd. A more comprehensive report on the subject is in preparation.

[13] For example, the World War II battle of the Sea of Bismarck is often used as an example of how game theory can help analyze combat decisions. See for example, O. G. Hayward, "Military Decision and Game Theory," *Journal of the Operations Research Society of America*, November 1954, Vol. 2 No. 4, pp 365–385. More recently, the same battle was discussed by Eric Rasmussen in *Games and Information*, 3rd ed., Oxford, UK: Blackwell, 2001.

In general, the success of a Blue military mission and the outcome of a Red attack depend on how well matched Red's strategy is to Blue's strategy.[14] Red must attack when and where Blue will travel and may need to adjust its tactics in a way that is tuned to the given Blue mission. We assume that the outcome of the game—or the fate of the mission—can be measured in terms of an expected payoff thought to be derived from the consequences of Red propaganda (sometimes referred to as the "CNN effect"), friendly casualties, and so on. Crucially, the analysis does not depend on actually measuring the payoffs. One approach is to examine relative payoffs. For example, Red may conclude that it has achieved its objective better with more Blue casualties than with fewer. The assumption is merely that the payoffs could be evaluated on some ordinal scale.

Figure 5.2 illustrates how Red-Blue interactions might be modeled as a noncooperative, two-player, zero-sum game. The game matrix

Figure 5.2
A Noncooperative Two-Sided Game

	Red			
	P_{11}	P_{12}	...	P_{1k}
	P_{21}	P_{22}	...	P_{2k}
Blue	...	...	...	...
	P_{n1}	P_{n2}	...	P_{nk}

RAND *MG682-5.2*

[14] Again, we are restricting our analysis to the military component of COIN in this case. Moreover, we further narrow the analysis to military operations against combatants and not against civilians or static targets.

entries, $P_{i,j}$, are the expected payoff of the mission outcome when Blue chooses strategy *i* and Red chooses strategy *j*. When planning missions, Blue makes decisions as described above. Therefore, the Blue strategy is a simultaneous choice of route, force size and composition, departure time, speed, inter-vehicle spacing, vehicle markings, and so on. Red, on the other hand, makes decisions about attacking Blue, and the Red strategy is therefore a simultaneous choice of attack site, time, tactics, munitions, and so on.

Any analysis of Red-Blue interactions requires assumptions, and an advantage of game theory is that it can provide a framework formaking those assumptions explicit. Table 5.2 enumerates some of the assumptions that might be required when applying game theory to study Red-Blue interactions in counterinsurgency operations.

Each assumption has operational significance that can be interpreted in the context of the game. Furthermore, the validity of these assumptions must be determined in the context of a specific game: It is easy to envision scenarios in which some of the assumptions *are not* true. The question is whether there are any interesting situations when all the assumptions *are* true, and how the outcome of the game changes when those assumptions are relaxed.

The primary strength of game theory for studying Red-Blue interactions in counterinsurgencies is that it offers a coherent analytical framework for thinking about the problem and for understanding how assumptions affect analysis. Game theory may be better suited to analysis at the strategic level, where details inherent to tactical-level engagement may be abstracted—i.e., where the assumptions may be a better approximation of reality.

The many assumptions needed to apply game theory make getting detailed tactical-level insights difficult. Indeed, the counterinsurgency faces a highly uncertain and dynamic environment; the nature of the game changes continuously as information flows around the battlefield. Moreover, instantiating the game in specific contexts may require data about tactical-level decisionmaking, which may be impractical because of the uncertainties and dynamics involved.

Table 5.2
Game Framework Assumptions

Assumption	Comments
Red can actually choose among its alternatives.	Choosing two or more options could be included as an additional Red strategy.
Blue can actually choose among its alternatives.	Choosing two or more options could be included as an additional Blue strategy.
Blue intelligence is slower than Red's decision cycle.	By implication, Blue must decide before observing Red's choice.
Red action time is greater than the time required to know Blue's choice.	By implication, Red must decide before observing Blue's choice.
Payoffs are zero-sum.	A Red reward is a Blue cost; a Blue reward is a Red cost.
The payoffs are known to both sides.	The payoff matrix is common knowledge.
The objective of the game is understood by both sides.	Options might be maximizing per-play average winnings; maximizing the frequency of repeated-play success; "bankrupting" the opponent in the course of repeated-play.
Red and Blue are the only players.	Different elements of the insurgency are not distinguished.

Finally, although game theory itself may not lead to direct insights, it may be used to develop hypotheses that can be tested empirically.

Response Detection

As we have often stated, insurgents are generally resourceful, and they adapt rapidly to changes in friendly-force tactics and technology. To better understand this dynamic, it is important to discern just what patterns the friendly forces are exhibiting that signal their intentions to the enemy. In addition, we need to know just how the enemy is exploiting those patterns before we can suggest how the patterns may be changed either to preclude enemy detection or to preclude enemy exploitation if preventing detection is not possible. One way to understand the Red-Blue interaction dynamic, and therefore to understand friendly behavior patterns and how they are exploited, is through the use of response detection techniques.

In a study currently being led by the Center for Naval Analyses (CNA), an iterative process is used that begins by examining a unit's historical movement patterns using archived BFT data.[15] The length of time examined will probably vary with the unit and the operational context. This is generally a graphical process whereby BFT data are plotted on a map of the unit's area of operation—outside its FOB. This is repeated for a subsequent time period of equal length and the difference is calculated—hence, the iterative nature of the process. In those areas where significant change is observed, analysis focuses on enemy activity to see how the enemy has exploited (responded to) the change in friendly behavior. Next, area density changes are computed within grids overlaid on the area of operations, and along road segments within those grids if more resolution is needed.

An important aspect of this type of analysis is the development of suitable measures and metrics that reflect the level of Red-Blue interaction from one time period to the next. For friendly forces, operational density is appropriate, i.e., the levels of Blue force activity per unit area or per unit kilometer. A suitable metric, then, is the amount of exposure Blue forces experience. By exposure, we mean the amount of time Blue forces spend outside the FOB (and are therefore exposed) per time period.[16] This leads to two metrics: hours off the FOB within the grid square in period i, and the hours spent on a road segment in the grid square during period i. If we assume there are n days in a period, and if we let $h_{i,j}$ = the number of hours Blue forces spent off the FOB in the grid square on day j, then the average density for the grid square for the period is

$$\bar{h}_i = \frac{1}{n}\sum_{j=1}^{n} h_{i,j}.$$

[15] The work presented here summarizes research conducted by Dr. Caryl Catarious, a research analyst at CNA. A more comprehensive report by Dr. Catarious is forthcoming. In addition, the U.S. Training and Doctrine Command Analysis Center at White Sands Missile Range has examined archived BFT data to calculate kilometers driven off the FOB versus time off the FOB.

[16] We have also used the distance traveled outside the FOB during the time period.

Similarly, the average density for each road segment within the grid is

$$\bar{l}_i = \frac{1}{n}\sum_{j=1}^{n} l_{i,j}\ .$$

For Red, the metrics are simply the activity of interest for the analysis being conducted. The SIGACTS databases in Iraq and Afghanistan, for example, contain information on all types of insurgent attacks. Consequently, such metrics as the number of friendly-force casualties per time period, the number of attacks of specific types or all types per time period, the number of weapons caches found and cleared per time period, etc., are all acceptable.[17] Like the Blue density metrics, we calculate similar Red density metrics for the period: $\bar{a}_i$ for the average enemy actions within the grid square for the period and $\bar{r}_i$ for the average enemy actions along the road segment for the period.

Next we develop a test statistic that assesses the level of Red-Blue interaction in period i and compare it to the same statistic in period $i+1$. We refer to this as the interaction ratio, and it is calculated to be $I_i = \bar{h}_i / \bar{a}_i$. We calculate a similar test statistic $L_i = \bar{l}_i / \bar{r}_i$ if needed (see the algorithmic process below). If I_i or L_i is "small," we conclude that the enemy is able to exploit the patterns the friendly forces are exhibiting. Consequently, tracking these statistics from period to period can highlight the effects of changes in Blue movement patterns within a grid or along a road segment. From all this, we state the null hypothesis $H_o : I_i - I_{i+1} = 0$. If this is rejected at some suitable level of confidence, we can then examine the reasons why. The response detection process proposed by CNA can be best presented as an algorithm.

Step 1. Create a graphical representation of friendly force activity within the unit's area of operation for the periods i and $i+1$. This is accomplished by plotting BFT data within grids superimposed on a map of the unit's area of operations. The intensity of traffic within a grid is then depicted visually by varying shades of a selected color (usually blue).

[17] Weapons caches found and cleared are not enemy activities, but the presence of caches is indicative of enemy activity and therefore it is included in this category.

Step 2. Subtract the densities in the period i map from the period $i+1$ map. This is accomplished by subtracting the hours the Blue unit spent in each grid during period i from the same thing for period $i+1$. This amounts to simple matrix subtraction. Once this has been accomplished, the resulting subtraction is again represented as a color-coded intensity plot.

Step 3. If the intensity resulting from the subtraction in the previous step (residual intensity) fails to exceed some threshold in at least one grid, increment i and go to Step 1.

Step 4. For those grids where the residual intensity does exceed some threshold, calculate the two test statistics, $I_i = \bar{h}_i / \bar{a}_i$, $I_{i+1} = \bar{h}_{i+1} / \bar{a}_{i+1}$ and test the hypothesis $H_o : I_i - I_{i+1} = 0$, as discussed above.[18]

Step 5. If the null hypothesis is not rejected, increment i and go to Step 1.

Step 6. For those grids where the null hypothesis is rejected, calculate the test statistic $L_i = \bar{l}_i / \bar{r}_i$, $L_{i+1} = \bar{l}_{i+1} / \bar{r}_{i+1}$, and test the hypothesis $H_o : L_i - L_{i+1} = 0$, as discussed above for each road segment in the grid.

Step 7. Because the change in grid intensity was significant, it is near certain that one or more of the road segment intensities will be as well. Record those for which the null hypothesis is rejected. Increment i and go to Step 1.

A second approach to analyzing response detection is to postulate the myriad possible Red responses in the form of a nonlinear equation with Red response as the dependent variable and Blue activity as the independent variable. We begin by proposing the following relationship between Red response and Blue activity:

---

[18] RAND colleague Thomas Sullivan developed a method for assessing the traffic density per unit time for each road segment in a grid. He also devised a visual response detection methodology for road segments similar to Dr. Catarious's area response methodology.

$$\bar{R} = \bar{B}^{\alpha}\left(1 - \bar{B}\right)^{\gamma},$$

where B is the amount of Blue activity in a grid or on a road segment and $\bar{B}$ is the normalized value of B so that $0 \le \bar{B} \le 1$. Similarly, R is the amount of Red response to Blue's activity in the same grid or road segment, and its normalized value is $0 \le \bar{R} \le 1$.[19] Normalizing Blue activity can be achieved by dividing the number of hours off the FOB in the time period by the total number of hours in the time period. Normalizing Red response is a bit more problematic. If R is measured in terms of the number of direct attacks against Blue, then a suitable normalizing function might be $\bar{R} = 1 - e^{-R}$.[20] For large numbers of attacks, $\bar{R}$ is also large (near 1) and the reverse is true for fewer attacks.

The advantage of this formulation is that it can model almost any Red response to Blue activity because the equation is essentially the Beta probability distribution defined on the interval [0,1]. The exponents α and γ are derived empirically using multiple regression techniques (more on this later), and the resulting curve is analyzed to discern how Red responds to Blue activity. The shape of the curve can provide insight to how Red might be resource constrained and thus it may provide critical information on how Blue might take advantage of it. Figure 5.3 illustrates the curves generated for four possible pairs of α and γ.

The first curve, $\alpha = 0.8$ and $\gamma = 0.3$, illustrates a case where Red responds to increasing Blue activity (presumably by increasing attackson Blue) but at a rather slow rate and only up to a certain point. Then, possibly because of resource constraints or operational exposure, Red decreases its attacks. The other curves have similar explanations. These examples are exemplary and are not based on any actual situation.

---

19 We drop the time period and grid reference subscripts here for ease of exposition.

20 See for example, Walter L. Perry, David Signori, and John E. Boon, Jr., *Exploring Information Superiority: A Methodology for Measuring the Quality of Information and Its Impact on Shared Awareness*, Santa Monica Calif.: RAND Corporation, MR 1467-OSD, 2004. In this work, the authors use the same exponential normalizer to assess the level of information quality.

Figure 5.3
Red-Blue Interaction Curves

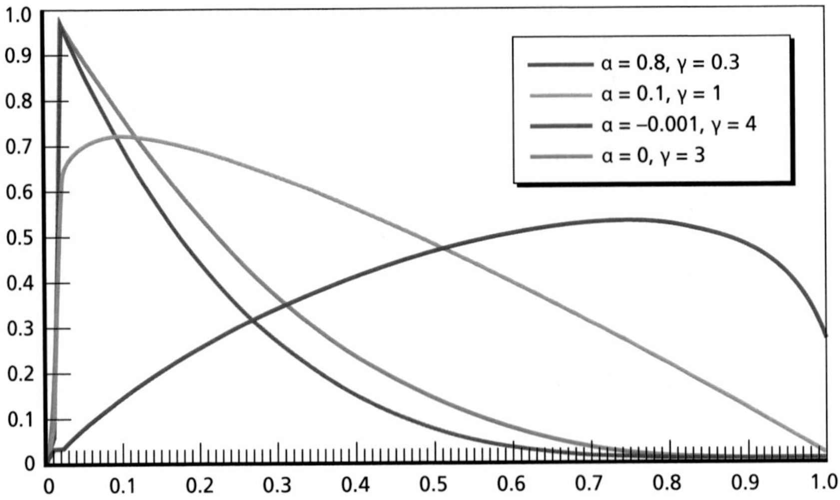

RAND *MG682-5.3*

Earlier, we alluded to empirically deriving estimates for α and γ using multiple regression techniques. As with the first change response method, we begin by postulating some period of time (*n* days) in which Blue and Red behavior is to be examined. We first gather the number of Red attacks and the number of Blue hours off the FOB for each of the *n* days, and normalize each as suggested above. By taking the logarithm of the Red-Blue interaction equation, we can then perform a linear multiple regression using the *n* days of data to produce estimates for α and γ. The resulting equation: $\log(\bar{R}) = \alpha \log(\bar{B}) + \gamma \log(1 - \bar{B})$ is in the appropriate regression format. With estimates for α and γ, we can create the appropriate curve for the given situation and then interpret its meaning much like the $\alpha = 0.8$ and $\gamma = 0.3$ case discussed above.

The goal of the response detection analysis is to focus on areas (grids or road segments) where (1) a significant change in Blue force activity has been observed and (2) insurgents have either successfully taken advantage of the change or have failed to take advantage of it. Regardless of the results, the next step is to understand the conditions under which the change took place: change in mission, increase (decrease) in the number of existing missions, increased time spent out of the FOB as in the current surge, more (or less) discernable patterns exhibited by Blue forces, and so on. In this way, the altered behavior of the force can be linked to the significant consequences, as illustrated by the statistical tests.

CHAPTER SIX

Conclusions

Our goal in this monograph has been to illustrate how operational analysis can be used to support counterinsurgency operations. Operational analysis has supported combat operations for quite some time.[1] In fact, operational research is generally thought to have begun in 1937 in the United Kingdom.

> . . . It began when, having developed radar, scientists were then asked to develop procedures for its use in a new, effective air defense system."[2]

Of course the application of mathematics to warfare predates operational analysis. Frederick Lanchester published his famous attrition model of combat in 1916.[3] So it is only natural to examine how analysis might support counterinsurgency operations. However, unlike conventional combat, in counterinsurgency, intelligence drives operations. Consequently, we have taken the position that analysis should focus on supporting intelligence operations. Indeed, the methods suggested above are all aimed at doing just that.

---

1 David Schrady, "Golden Anniversary: Fifty Years of Graduate Education at [Naval Postgraduate School] NPS Produces 3,300 Alumni Worldwide," *ORMS Today*, February, 2001.

2 Harold Larnder, "The Origins of Operational Research," in *Operations Research*, Vol. 32, No. 2, March–April, 1984.

3 Fredrick William Lanchester, "Mathematics in Warfare," in *The World of Mathematics*, Redmond, Wash.: Tempus Books, 1956.

Modern Insurgency

Insurgencies evolve over time. Normally starting as a small, clandestine movement of "true believers," insurgent movements are usually very weak and vulnerable in their initial—proto-insurgency—stage. Indeed, most fail in this stage. If the movement survives and begins to grow, it has the potential of becoming a large-scale insurgency with a reasonable chance of succeeding. During this evolution, the role of government security agencies changes, too. Whereas the police and intelligence agencies have a leading role initially, as the insurgency worsens the military begins to move to the forefront, since the police can no longer cope with the situation. Critically, much of the counterinsurgency effort and approach, especially early in the insurgency, is closer to police work than it is to conventional military operations—hence, the primacy of intelligence operations.

Our understanding of modern insurgency is evolving and improving. In some respects, the lessons and techniques used in past counterinsurgency efforts remain valid today. In other areas, important changes have taken place, especially in the ability of insurgents to use modern global information and communications networks to recruit, spread propaganda, organize, and control their operations.

It seems certain that for the future, the United States and its allies will confront enemies operating on a scale similar to insurgencies. That is, faced with the conventional superiority of arms, future enemies will undoubtedly resort to tactics similar to what we have observed in Iraq and Afghanistan. Consequently, there will be a continuing need for a body of analytic techniques that can be used to support counterinsurgency-like operations.

The Role of Analysis

As analysts engaged in trying to understand and assess modern insurgencies, we must realize that this form of conflict differs from what we grew accustomed to during the Cold War and the 1990s, when most of us focused on the interaction of conventional military forces. We have seen that instead of conducting operational analysis, we are really engaged in using operational analysis techniques to support intelligence operations.

The techniques we have suggested include social network analysis to understand connections between the insurgent groups and within groups; pattern recognition techniques to reduce factors contributing to insurgence violence to a few indicators; predictive and forecasting techniques to help determine likely sites of future violence; and game theory to examine the relative strategies of Red and Blue with respect to counterinsurgency objectives. We have also suggested the use of change detection techniques focused on the effects of changes in Blue operating patterns on Red attack activity.

As with all analysis, good results depend heavily on the data used. Beyond the difficulties associated with data in counterinsurgency operations that we have outlined, however, other questions inevitably arise: Is the right kind of information being sought and archived by the friendly forces at each stage of the insurgency? How is that information being processed and shared—especially with the analytic community? What about timely sharing among multiple agencies, including among multinational partners? Finally, as the insurgents adapt and change, is the intelligence-operations process of the friendly forces changing accordingly?

Bibliography

Beckett, Ian F. W., and John Pimlott, *Armed Forces & Modern Counter-Insurgency,* Sydney: Croom Helm Ltd., 1985.

Boot, Max, *The Savage Wars of Peace, Small Wars and the Rise of American Power,* New York: Basic Books, 2002.

Byman, Daniel, *Understanding Proto-Insurgencies,* RAND Counterinsurgency Study—Paper 3, Santa Monica, Calif.: RAND Corporation, OP-178-OSD, 2007. As of February 26, 2008:
http://www.rand.org/pubs/occasional_papers/OP178/

Byman, Daniel, Peter Chalk, Bruce Hoffman, William Rosenau, and David Brannan, *Trends in Outside Support for Insurgent Movements,* Santa Monica, Calif.: RAND Corporation, MR-1405-OTI, 2001. As of February 26, 2008:
http://www.rand.org/pubs/monograph_reports/MR1405/

Cordesman, Anthony H., *The Lessons of Modern War,* Volume III, London: Mansell Publishing Ltd., 1990.

Field Manual (FM) 3-24 and Marine Corps Warfighting Publication (MCWP) 3-33.5, *Counterinsurgency,* Washington, D.C.: Headquarters, Department of the Army and Headquarters, United States Marine Corps, December 2006.

Gompert, David C., *Heads We Win: The Cognitive Side of Counterinsurgency (COIN):* RAND Counterinsurgency Study—Paper 1, Santa Monica, Calif.: RAND Corporation, OP-168-OSD, 2007. As of February 26, 2008:
http://www.rand.org/pubs/occasional_papers/OP168/

Gordon, A. D., *Classification,* 2nd ed., New York: Chapman and Hall, 1999.

Hayward, O. G., Jr., "Military Decision and Game Theory," *Journal of the Operations Research Society of America,* November 1954, Vol. 2, No. 4, pp 365–385.

Hollywood, John, Thomas Sullivan, Ryan Keefe, David Nealy, and Walter L. Perry, *Targeting IED Networks in Iraq,* Santa Monica, Calif.: RAND Corporation, forthcoming. Not releasable to the general public.

Joes, Anthony J., *Resisting Rebellion: The History and Politics of Counterinsurgency,* Lexington, Ky.: University of Kentucky Press, 2004.

Kulldorff, Martin, "Spatial Scan Statistics: Models, Calculations, and Applications," in *Scan Statistics and Applications,* Joseph Glaz and N. Balakrishnan (eds.), Boston, Mass.: Birkhäuser, 1999, pp. 303–322.

Lanchester, Fredrick William, "Mathematics in Warfare," in *The World of Mathematics,* Redmond, Wash.: Tempus Books, 1956.

Larnder, Harold, "The Origins of Operational Research," in *Operations Research,* Vol. 32, No. 2, March–April, 1984

MacQueen, James B., "Some Methods for Classification and Analysis of Multivariate Observations," *Proceedings of the 5th Berkeley Symposium on Mathematical Statistics and Probability,* Vol. 1, pp. 281–297, Berkeley, Calif.: University of California Press, 1967.

Magnuson, Stewart, "Adaptive Foe Thwarts Counter-IED Efforts," *National Defense,* January 2006. As of on June 4, 2007: http://www.nationaldefensemagazine.org/issues/2006/jan/adaptive_foe.htm

Meigs, Montgomery C., *Slide Rules and Submarines,* Washington, D.C.: National Defense University Press, 1990.

Nagl, John A., *Learning to Eat Soup with a Knife, Counterinsurgency Lessons from Malaya and Vietnam,* Chicago: University of Chicago Press, 2002.

Operational Analysis and the Counter-IED Fight, Briefing by the U.S. Joint IED Defeat Organization, March 2007.

Perry, Walter L., David Signori, and John E. Boon, Jr, *Exploring Information Superiority: A Methodology for Measuring the Quality of Information and Its Impact on Shared Awareness,* Santa Monica Calif.: RAND Corporation, MR 1467-OSD, 2004. As of February 26, 2008: http://www.rand.org/pubs/monograph_reports/MR1467/

Predd, Joel, "On-Line Learning and IEDs: Exploring the Possibilities," RAND Briefing, November 2006.

Rasmussen, Eric, *Games and Information,* 3rd ed., Oxford, UK: Blackwell, 2001.

Schrady, David, "Golden Anniversary: Fifty years Of Graduate Education at [Naval Postgraduate School] NPS Produces 3,300 Alumni Worldwide," *ORMS Today,* February, 2001. As of May 29, 2007: http://www.lionhrtpub.com/orms/orms-2-01/nps.html

Stanton, Shelby L., *The Rise and Fall of an American Army, U.S. Ground Forces in Vietnam, 1965–1973.* Novato, Calif.: Presidio Press, 1985.

Sullivan, Thomas, and Walter L. Perry, "Identifying Indicators of Chemical, Biological, Radiological and Nuclear (CBRN) Weapons Development Activity in Sub-National Terrorist Groups," *Journal of the Operational Research Society*, Vol. 55, 2004, pp. 361–374.

Wilson, Alyson G., Gregory D. Wilson, and David H. Olwell, eds., *Statistical Methods in Counterterrorism: Game Theory, Modeling, Syndromic Surveillance, and Biometric Authentication*, New York: Springer, 2006.